The Case Against Marriage
What You're Really Getting. What You've Got To Lose

By Glenn Campbell

Geoaktif Publications

First Geoaktif Edition
Geoaktif Publications
Atıf Yılmaz Cad. No: 16 Kat:4 Beyoglu-Istanbul/TURKEY
Tel: ++90 212 244 85 63 E-mail: bilgi@geoaktifyayinlari.com
Web: www.geoaktifyayinlari.com

For information on this book and additional links, see:
http://CaseAgainstMarriage.com

Preface

Greetings, voyager!

You are new to this planet, as are we all, and you still have much to learn. No matter how old you may be, you are probably heading down roads you have not traveled before. Others may have described these roads, but there is much you must learn for yourself. Do not make the mistake of thinking all your mistakes are behind you. You have quite a few yet to come, and I am here to try to wave you off from one or two.

In this collection of essays and observations, I am trying to build a case for an unpopular position. Some would call me a cynic or a misanthrope, trying to devalue the warm and genuine feelings people have for each other. Others would say I am working against the will of God. If a certain way of life has stood by our people for generations, why should we change it now? What sort of person would question 10,000 years of human history?

Some would claim that I do not believe in love, but that is not true. I am trying to defend love from the delusions and social conventions that get in its way. I am trying to surgically separate that which is love from that which only seems to be love but actually poisons it. Love can be proven only when it is freely given, not when it is coerced or enforced by outside pressure. I am trying to carve off the coercion and leave love itself intact.

Indulge me, if you will, and let me express my absurd ideas.

You have nothing to lose! If I raise objections and you can counter them comfortably with your own arguments, you have grown stronger. On the other hand, if I plant a seed of doubt in your mind, perhaps it is something you ought to deal with. Maybe this little bit of disturbing news could save you a whole lot of grief in the long run.

Do not make the mistake of killing the messenger before you have heard the message. Don't shoot me, please! Let me speak first. Let me get all the unpleasant news out in the open. *Then* you can shoot me.

Glenn Campbell, Las Vegas

Introduction

You are probably not going to listen to me, but I am going to give it a shot anyway. You have been considering marriage, and I am here to dissuade you. I'm not against love, mind you, or even against bonding for life if that's the way things turn out. It is only the public contract I object to. Why does a private relationship need a public sanction? Why can't you negotiate your relationship on your own, as it unfolds, just between the two of you, without the social or governmental license?

Instead of enhancing your relationship, marriage might screw it up permanently, replacing true attraction with a dull institution. At the least, it reduces your flexibility, making it harder to respond to inevitable changes in yourself and your partner.

There are plenty of married people out there, and I am not saying they should get unmarried. We all have to make the best of our current circumstances. I only want to address you, the naïve young dilettante, while there is still a chance to save you.

Let us think this thing through together, shall we? What does marriage really mean, and what are its practical effects? Is it really going to help your relationship or hurt it? What are the legal, social, economic and psychological ramifications of walking down the aisle? Why do people think they need marriage, and how are they deluded?

Gays and lesbians are often complaining because they

cannot get married in many jurisdictions. I say they should count their blessings! It is like women fighting for the right to join the military and go to war. Before you make a big deal about it, you ought to think through the personal implications: "Do I really want to go to war?" Why should gays fight to join the same prison everyone else is trapped in?

Gay relationships, in fact, may be leading the way to an enlightened future that heterosexuals ought to embrace. Think about it: If gay couples cannot legally marry, what do they do? They piece together the elements of marriage *á la carte*, deliberately, as it suits their needs. If they want to share death benefits, they make up wills. If they want to share a bank account, they open one together. They don't try to share *everything* all at once from this day forth, which, legally, is what marriage makes you do. Gays have to negotiate every act of sharing on a case-by-case basis, which is the essence of a healthy and dynamic relationship. In the absence of specific negotiated sharing, they remain free and independent individuals.

I know something about marriage from having been there once. I have also seen the tail end of the institution as an unofficial observer of Family Court in Las Vegas. Las Vegas, of course, is the marriage capital of the world, but you learn far more about the institution by studying divorces as they pass through court. There is a Yin and Yang between marriage and divorce. The first thing I learned in Family Court is that the nastiness of the divorce is proportional to the unreality of the original delusion. You can't fall madly in love without expecting to fall just as madly out. Divorce proves that nothing is free in life, even if love seems to offer it.

When you go through a divorce, there is plenty of blame floating around, but in the end, you have to acknowledge that it was your own damn fault. You were the one who bought into this fantasy. Before you got married, you believed the fairytale nonsense—that marriage was really going to change your relationship for the better and make it more "secure." Security cuts both ways: In trying to lock out the uncertainties of the world, you are locking yourself in a cage that reduces your freedom. Because you can no longer easily step away, you may have lost much of your ability to negotiate with your cellmate. Instead, you make accommodations and more accommodations and sweep problems under the carpet until—Kaboom!—things finally blow up.

The urge to merge with someone else can be huge, but there is a practical limit to how far you can go. If you get too close to anyone for too long, there are bound to be problems. It is like being handcuffed to the one you love: After the novelty wears off, it is going to be a pain to get anything done. The person you are trapped with is bound to fray on your nerves. Once you have already shared everything you can share, you hunger for new experiences as an independent being so you can maybe come back later and share again.

The healthiest base position is one of discrete individuality. We should each be self-contained entities with our own careers, assets, goals and relationships. We should come together with others only as it suits us, negotiating each engagement on its own merits. Over time, we might share more of ourselves, and this is fine, as long as it happens naturally. You never have to take any "Big Step" to make a relationship work. Instead, a lot of little steps could conceivably lead you to the same result. If you negotiate your boundaries slowly and incrementally, what you will probably have in the end is a more solid and stable relationship, because everything was carefully built stone by stone to suit your needs, not purchased as a prefabricated unit built for everyone else.

The institution of marriage replaces an independently constructed relationship with a single social contract that attempts to compact years of development into a single two-word sentence: "I do." It is a waving of the magic wand that is supposed to build everything all at once. It is like buying your diploma from a mail order company rather than actually going to college. You stand before all your family and friends and say, "This is all I am ever going to want for the rest of my life." Do you think that by saying this you are really going to make it happen?

If it does happen—if you do remain attached to each other for life—how do you know it was really a free choice? Did you stay together because it was truly the best arrangement, or was it because you were imprisoned together and escape was too painful? If you are married, you are never really going to know.

In this book, we will explore marriage, relationships, sexual attraction, law, contracts, loneliness and fear. What are people afraid of when they get married? No institution can be all positive; there have to be demons under the surface, and we will try our best to dig them up.

What is Marriage?

What is marriage?

This may seem like a complicated question. There are many dimensions to it: emotional, sexual, religious, cultural, financial. If you ask a hundred people on the street what marriage is, you are probably going to get a hundred different answers.

However, if you ask a hundred *lawyers* the same question, you are more likely to get a consensus. Under the law, marriage is quite simple: It is an economic contract to share future income and liabilities. You can layer on top of it whatever emotional meaning you want, but what the law sees is primarily a merging of your economic activity.

Under the law, marriage creates a new economic entity called the marital "community." This is a common pot that both of you are contributing to and taking from. The exact legal mechanism differs by state and country, but getting married anywhere implies that you are going to merge the major portion of your money and property into one corporate entity. As far as the law is concerned, you will cease to be independent economic beings.

In "community property" states like Nevada, the distribution is simple and brutally rational. Unless you have an explicit written agreement otherwise, everything you and your spouse earn "from this day forth" is going into the community pot, regardless of whose name is attached to it. Everything bought with this money is community property that the two of you jointly own, even if it can only be realistically used by one party or the other. At the same time, any new debt incurred by one member of the community is automatically borne in equal proportion by the other.

After you are married, you may think you still have your own checking account, credit cards, clothing and possessions, but under the law, this separate ownership is fiction. The only things you still own by yourself are those you acquired before the wedding. Everything accrued after it belongs to the community.

(In "common law" states, things work a little differently. In that case, a married partner can "own" a piece of property by themselves, but their spouse is still entitled to a slice of it at the time of the divorce.)

At the time of your marriage, you may think of the community as something benign and protective, but it can easily turn into a monster. Instead of being financially responsible only for yourself, you are now responsible for a person who you may have only limited control over. Yes, you can benefit from their good fortune, but you can also face enormous personal losses from their misfortune that may persist long after they are gone.

Financially, marriage can be seen as erasing a firewall of protection between the two of you. Any financial disease that is contracted by one is automatically contracted by the other. If you remain unmarried and simply share whatever you choose to, you incur no such downside risk. You do not have to be married to someone to help support them; you can give another person any portion of your assets any time you want, just like gifts to a friend. All that marriage adds is the legal *obligation* to support your partner and help dig them out of any bad financial decisions they make by themselves.

You may not fully realize the significance of the community

until the time of your divorce. Once the common pot has been created, the law has little interest in who contributes what. If you work hard for ten years while your partner sits on his/her derrière eating bonbons, they are still entitled (in a community property state) to half of everything you earned. Furthermore, through a draconian but legally logical feature called "alimony," you may be required to pay them a continuing stipend after the divorce for any discrepancy in your incomes.

Here is a worst case scenario: Let's say you get married and go to Las Vegas for your honeymoon (evidently because you lack imagination). The day following your wedding, your spouse goes on a gambling and buying spree and maxes out *his own* credit cards. Unfortunately, his debt is now your debt, because it was incurred after your wedding. At the time of your eventual divorce, the newly acquired debt is going to be split 50-50 regardless of who was responsible.

As another extreme example, imagine your spouse gets cancer, exceeds the limits of his or her health insurance coverage and starts racking up enormous hospital bills. You are responsible for paying those bills even after your spouse dies, whereas you would have no financial liability if you had only lived with them and never married.

At the wedding ceremony, everybody talks about all the good things you are going to share. No one talks about the bad things. On the upside, if your spouse gets rich, so do you in equal measure. On the downside, if your spouse gets sued, you are automatically the codefendant. Your potential liability, sharing in your partner's financial fate, is as unlimited as the potential reward.

The legal concept of shared property was created for good reason. Once upon a time, the primary purpose of marriage was the rearing of children. Sex was prohibited outside of marriage because it inevitably produced babies who needed to be raised in a stable and socially sanctioned environment.

Marriage was the joining of one man and one woman into a single child-rearing unit. The woman stayed at home to manage the hearth, while the man went out into the woods and brought home dinner.

Even if she didn't actually do the hunting, the woman was entitled to a share of everything her husband brought home. This was only fair. It was the woman and her children who were the most vulnerable. If a wife struggled to maintain her husband's home for many years, then the husband struck it rich, the husband couldn't just say, "See you later!" The husband's good fortune was automatically the wife's. Unfortunately, legal logic meant the system also worked the other way around: The husband's debts were also the wife's.

Our current marriage and divorce laws have arisen from this medieval background, even though social conditions have changed since then. The wide availability of contraception in the late 20th Century totally rewrote the rules of the marriage game. People today do not necessarily get married because they expect to have children; instead, they are seeking some sort of emotional satisfaction. They may dismiss the whole financial merging as insignificant, but it is still there—the same as in medieval times—and it is the main thing the law cares about at the time of divorce.

Whereas procreation used to be inevitable in most marriages (and a humiliating curse if it didn't happen), emotional satisfaction is much more unreliable. The modern quest for "happiness" is difficult to define and nearly impossible to pin down. While children are going to stick around for years, emotional satisfaction can evaporate in an instant. When happiness vanishes in a modern marriage, divorce is more likely than it used to be, and you face the messy problem of dividing up that medieval community pot.

Once upon a time, people bonded for life. This notion may sound romantic at first, as though this kind of loyalty was a lost art. Then you realize that "life" in the supposedly romantic Middle Ages was usually brutal and very short. Most people were too busy surviving and procreating to think about emotional concerns. If your expected lifespan was 40 years and you saw death all around you, you had to make children fast! There may or may not have been period of courtship before the wedding ceremony, but if there was, it was a naive and idealistic romance of supervised walks in the park undiluted by the real experience of, say, living with someone for a few months. After the marriage, the courtship was over, and there wasn't much time for emotion thereafter.

Most people in the modern world are "serial bonders." As the human lifespan increases and the pre-contraception generation passes away, it is increasingly difficult to find anyone who has truly "bonded for life," even though they may claim it for their current relationship. Instead, people bond for a few years, usually believing they have bonded for life but eventually falling out of it. This isn't so unreasonable when people are living 80+ years instead of 40. In the modern world, people have the time and opportunity to grow and change, and the relationship that was right in one phase of your life may not be best for the next.

In developed countries in 21st Century, the legal institution of marriage still persists in its medieval form but with one very important change: It has been almost entirely separated from sex and procreation. These days in most Western countries you can engage in fornication with impunity, no license required, and can live with your partner without anyone's permission. You no longer have to wait for your wedding night to enjoy the forbidden fruit of sex. Now, that fruit is available *á la carte*. Modern marriage grants you no special sexual privilege.

Contrary to popular belief, marriage is *not* a parenting contract. The real parenting contract, as far as modern courts are concerned, is the child's birth certificate. Regardless of whether the parents are married, it is the birth certificate that determines who has parental rights and is jointly responsible the child's well-being. (If the birth certificate shows no father, then a DNA test is usually the determining factor—something medieval courts did not have access to.) If child custody and child support are decided at the time of divorce, it is mainly a matter of judicial convenience. When the economic relationship has collapsed, it is assumed that the parenting relationship also has, but they are essentially governed by separate legal systems.

However you may define marriage, most of its long-term power—for better or worse—derives from the simple sharing of economic assets and liabilities. Presumably, you are willing to share all of your finances with someone because you trust them and expect to live with them forever. Once you start down this road, disentangling this arrangement becomes messier with time, and this exerts its own emotional pressure on the relationship. From a logistical standpoint—let alone emotional—divorce is many times more difficult than, say, preparing your taxes or planning your original wedding. Your natural fear of this massive bureaucratic challenge may be enough to convince you that your relationship is working even if it isn't.

Since the main purpose of marriage is no longer the raising of children but the seeking of something emotional, the big question is whether creating the community pot really increases the likelihood that your emotional goals will be achieved. If you are seeking only to be happier, how does combining your financial accounts serve this goal?

Happiness—isn't that what every decision is about nowadays? When you start down any road, aren't you choosing it because it promises you some sort of greater satisfaction than you have now? Otherwise, why bother to change course at all? What exactly is this happiness people are after? What does it look like? How does it work? Marriage aside, what are people trying to address when they enter into a long-term relationship? When you dream about romance, what are you really seeking?

Pair Bonding

"Bonding" is the process by which humans become emotionally attached to one another. It is like tying two people together with an invisible rope. When you are bonded to someone, you are always drawn back to them, whether or not the relationship is healthy for you.

Two kinds of bonding are critical to the survival of our species: the bond between child and parent and that between the man and woman in a child-rearing unit. A toddler won't wander very far from his parents; he may explore for a few minutes on his own, but then he looks around with alarm. "Where's Mom?" he says with a touch of fear, and he runs back to her. Likewise, a man who goes out into the world to hunt for food for his mate is drawn to return to her and not just wander off. (Oh, there may be some delays and diversions, but the woman can trust he will be back, with a damn good excuse for why he was late!)

If you are bonded to someone and are separated from them for a while, you start getting anxious. Toddlers cry for their parents, and adults start calling on their mobile phones just to hear the voice of their partner. What is said on the phone doesn't matter a whole lot. Both toddlers and lovers just want to assure themselves that their relationship is still secure.

Bonding can work in both directions or just one: The person you are bonded to can be equally attached to you or might not even know you exist. A teenager can become bonded to a heartthrob movie star who definitely can't return the sentiment, but the bond is still real to the teen. When a bond exists in only one direction, we call it "unrequited love."

Bonding is a physiological and neurological imprinting process involving a primitive and unconscious part of the brain. The thinking part of the brain doesn't have a lot to do with it. An infant is going to become bonded to whoever is taking care of him. He doesn't stop to think, "Is this the best parent for me?" Likewise, if a man and a woman are shipwrecked on a desert island together, they are probably going to become emotionally attached to each other regardless of the healthiness of the relationship.

The lesson here is you have to be careful which desert island you let yourself be shipwrecked on! Once you are there and the bonds start to form, things get complicated. Couples create their own desert islands. You know how lovers are: They look into each other's eyes and completely block off the rest of the world. It is both joyful and a little scary, because once you become bonded to one partner someone better for you can stand right in front of you and you won't even see them.

The existence of a neurological bond between two people does not imply that the relationship is healthy. Sometimes it is just blind addiction. People can be bonded to each other who have nothing else in common and who even openly hate each other. This is why some former romantic partners turn violent. All functional aspects of the relationship may have collapsed, but the primitive attachment is still engraved in the recesses of the brain. Instead of phoning to say how much they love the other person, the frustrated party can call to issue threats and to try to engage the other in a fight. This, too, is an expression of bonding.

In the animal kingdom, humans are classified as "pair bonded" creatures. The natural order of things seems to be one man bonding with one woman for long periods. Even for homosexuals, pair bonding seems to be a desirable outcome sought by most. It is extremely rare to find someone of any sexual persuasion who doesn't care to bond at all. There are plenty of single adults in the world, but most of them remain single mainly because the circumstances for bonding haven't been right, not because of a lack of private desire.

Statistically, most humans end up pair-bonded sooner or later. If this is the lifestyle that people naturally gravitate toward, there is no reason to fight it. The problem is finding the right person to bond with, one who enhances one's potential rather than drawing it down. Once the bond has been formed, the problem is how to make the relationship work in a complex modern environment. This is something that is not coded in the genes and doesn't necessarily come naturally.

In ancient marriage systems, still practiced in some parts of the world, who bonds with whom is considered far too important to be left to the parties themselves. After puberty, boys and girls are kept strictly segregated, and the elders alone determine who will be placed on a desert island together.

Victims of arranged marriages will bond just as surely as those who marry for love. Choosing your own spouse may be no predictor of long-term success—at least if you count "success" as the absence of divorce. Proponents of arranged marriages in modern India point out that their rate of divorce is much lower than in the Western world. In both arranged and chosen marriages, the relationship can turn dour and loveless with time. The difference in Western cultures is probably a greater willingness to jump ship when you are unhappy.

Western culture emphasizes the notion of romance as an avenue for personal happiness and enhancement, not procreation. If producing and raising children is your only goal, then almost any partner will do, as long as they bring home the bacon or are ready to bear fruit. If, on the other hand, you are looking for some kind of vague personal satisfaction, your standards are much higher—maybe impossibility high. In a sense, producing children is far easier than finding happiness, which is an endlessly shifting target.

Pair bonding is a neurological latching-on to the other person. The formation of this bond usually goes by the term of "falling in love." Bond formation can be a joyous experience! Everything about your partner becomes magical: their look, their smell, the color of their eyes. Everything they do seems so very fascinating! It feels, for a while, like there is no one else in the universe and that you were somehow "made for each other." People who have to watch this gooey lovefest from the outside may feel a little queasy, but to you it is the most wonderful feeling in the world.

The dreamy unreality of falling in love is really the brain rearranging itself to absorb this new image of "Mom." After a while, the fog lifts; objects become solid again, and you have reached your destination. Bonded! Now what do you do?

Sex becomes irrelevant very quickly. Just like any other bodily pleasure, the neurological reward is bound to diminish with time. Eventually, sex is more like a routine maintenance activity than meaningful communication. Sexual attraction is replaced by a non-sexual bond more like that between parent and child. Even if you married the perfect sexual specimen, you eventually stop seeing their body and it becomes no more special to you than your own. Instead, you become preoccupied with the routine problems of living. After the bond stabilizes, it is taken for granted. A new family is formed, and the two of you are less like lovers and more like a couple of siblings who have been sharing the same bedroom since as long as you can remember.

This is when the real trials emerge. Back in your courtship days, sexual attraction and your own desperate emotional need inevitably censored the differences and inconsistencies between the two of you. "Sure, he's a convicted serial killer," you said, "but I can change him." As the sensual attraction wanes, those practical problems, previously swept under the carpet, reemerge with a vengeance and have to be dealt with. It is a huge challenge. You thought that falling in love was going to solve all of your problems; instead, it just gave you new ones.

Withdrawing from a bonded relationship can be very difficult and painful. It is similar to trying to quit an addiction, because addiction and love come from the same place in the brain. Even if you have made the decision that the relationship isn't working, your partner might not have reached the same conclusion. Webs of dependency have developed and egos are on the line, so it may not be possible to pull away gracefully. Separation is going to be many times more difficult if your finances have been merged and you have made a public vow to stay with this person "forever." Aren't you a person of your word? How can you go back on it?

As the songs say, "Breaking up is hard to do." In popular culture, when someone is "dumped" by their girlfriend or boyfriend, it is an emblem of loserhood. It could be the worst part of your week! The damage, however, is mainly to your ego, and you will quickly recover—if you were never married. Divorce, however, can be absolutely devastating. It is not just an ego problem or a de-bonding problem but a vast surgical challenge, like separating conjoined twins. All your financial accounts, joined at once on your wedding day and built upon for years, have to be fairly divided.

Aren't the dilemmas of bonding difficult enough without adding these additional layers?

Sex and Intimacy

All of us are sexual creatures. It is programmed into us by our genes. Sex is obviously needed for procreation, but humans exhibit far more lust than can be explained by reproduction alone. Sex is also a bonding mechanism. It is part of the emotional "glue" that holds couples together during the long commitment required to raise a child to adulthood.

Sex may make sense from an evolutionary standpoint, but from the viewpoint of an adolescent just discovering it, it seems bizarre and disturbing. If you analyze sex too rationally, it's Loony Tunes! "Gross!" kids say when they first learn the functional details. It makes no logical sense for men to drool over Playboy models merely for their arrangement of fat deposits or for women to lust after... whatever it is women lust after. (You tell me!) Sex may be biologically sensible, but it doesn't make sense in the rational models of behavior we have been taught to live by.

As you make fateful decisions about your own life, your sex drive is bound come into conflict with the thinking part of your brain. Obeying your sexual feelings blindly can lead to some very unhappy results—if not prison—so your animal drives have to be moderated and disciplined by your intellect. Nonetheless, the sex drive is there, and no one can totally ignore it.

Unless you believe Freud, children are asexual until puberty. At that point a seemingly alien mechanism kicks in:

They begin to be drawn lasciviously to the opposite gender (or maybe to the same gender). These sensations are visceral, not rational. Boys don't make a logical decision that they like breasts and want to see and touch them. For that matter, girls don't have any choice about growing breasts or being drawn to guys. The whole change is a frightening Frankenstein experiment—with you being the monster!

Just because you are drawn to the opposite sex doesn't mean you know what to do with them! Dogs bark at cars without a clue what to do if they caught one. It may take adolescents a few years to connect the inexplicable feelings inside them to a desire for sexual intercourse. They can be attracted to the opposite sex even when they still think sex itself is gross. When they do understand that sexual attraction draws them toward the sexual act, intercourse itself doesn't really provide much resolution. After you finally have sex with the one you are attracted to, what do you do with them?

Sexual attraction can be very cruel that way: It starts pushing you along a certain path but gives you no further instructions. It might tell you how to start a relationship, but it doesn't tell you how to maintain one. Once the attraction is triggered, people don't just want coitus. They have complex emotional expectations for the relationship that are often self-contradictory and may or may not be fulfillable.

You can think of sex as a useful catalyst that can help get an intimate relationship started but that cannot sustain a relationship on its own. This catalyst may bring people together but it doesn't tell them what to do next. For that, you have to call on a whole new set of skills that have nothing to do with sex.

What do people really want from romantic relationships? They are looking for self-worth, purpose and relief from their loneliness. They are "existential" problems—meaning that they arise as a natural product of our existence on earth. As powerful as sexual attraction may be, it pales beside people's struggle with who they are and why they are here. These are problems that we may think a relationship will solve but that it can't.

Life, by its nature, is lonely and confusing. We appear on this planet in bodies that are alien to us, living with a family we did not choose, with no instruction manual or pre-mission briefing. As we outgrow our family, we discover that we are largely insignificant characters in a world that cares little about us. The myths about life we were given as children stop working. The simple universe where justice was provided by Mom and Dad gives way to a more complicated one where no one seems to be in charge. Who will take care of us now?

With a romantic relationship, we hope to fill this void. We dream of someone who loves us unconditionally the way our first caregiver did. We want a trusted confidante with whom we can share our innermost thoughts and feelings. We want someone who will take care of us when we are ill and protect us from danger. We want someone to praise us for our successes and maybe even worship us, but we also want them to give us direction and tell us what to do.

There may not be anyone on earth who can provide all these services! Furthermore, we may not be secure enough in ourselves to accept this person even if they walked in the door right now. Whether our dreams are achievable does not prevent us from having those fantasies whenever we pass a hottie on the street. The monkey part of our brain says, "Mmmmm, want sex!" but then the higher existential part kicks in and wants to know whether this person will fill all the other empty holes within us.

No relationship can fill up all our empty holes, but as long as we don't expect it to, a romantic engagement may still be worthwhile. Even if the existential problems are our own to solve, there is still value in intimacy.

What is intimacy? Intimacy is an intuitive channel of communication between two people who know each other very well. Instead of needing twenty words to say something, you can do it in only one or two—or maybe no words at all! Intimacy involves having a shared language and a body of common experience that help you convey more subtle meanings than you can share with anyone else.

Intimacy is valuable because it gives you another set of eyes, ears and mental judgments. It's like having a second brain. Whenever you go off track, your intimate partner can presumably tell you so. Intimate communication is never perfect, and there will always be some gaps in communication, but it can relieve at least some of your loneliness by giving you someone to talk to about your problems.

Intimacy is inherently non-sexual, but sex can be used to get it started. There can be huge natural barriers between individuals, and sex may be the only mechanism that can overcome them. Sex at least creates temporary physical intimacy. Emotional and intellectual intimacy may flow from it, but only if the parties are mature and motivated enough to build it.

Once intimacy is achieved, it is a precious treasure that needs to be protected. True intimacy is very fragile and can be easily lost. Intimacy is based on trust, and once trust slips away, the communication channel closes down. When that happens, you are no longer saying what you really think but what you think is necessary to keep the peace. After a while, you may find yourself going through the empty motions of intimacy without actually exchanging any information.

If intimacy is the most valuable element of a relationship, shouldn't this be what we are focusing on? In a long-term relationship, sex becomes inconsequential, as does the public image of the relationship projected to others. All that really matters is how well you and your partner are communicating and the value of what you say.

The conventional wisdom of marriage is that if you trap people together, making it more difficult to escape, they have to make the relationship work because they have no choice. Does this theory really make sense? Is imprisonment the best way to encourage and maintain intimacy?

Two people trapped on a desert island can get to know each other's habits very well, but that doesn't mean they trust each other or can talk to each other. Without trust, you are not going to reveal too much of your inner life. In reality, two people trapped on a desert island can come to distrust and dislike each other a great deal! At that point, the healthy solution for both is to get off the island and away from each other.

If you prevent them from leaving, is that going to make intimacy easier or just harden their dysfunction?

Loneliness and Engulfment

Once you start falling in love, the big question is, where do you stop?

No one wants to be lonely. It can be terrible to think no one cares about you, understands you or needs you. When the opportunity for love comes along, you may dive in. It can be a wonderful feeling to melt into the arms of another. Deeper and deeper you drift into their warm embrace, until you wake up in a panic....

"I can't breathe!"

Inside each of us are two conflicting forces. One is the "urge to merge"—a desire to join with others, to love and be loved and to become part of a team. The opposing force is "differentiation"—the desire to be a valuable, powerful and independent person in your own right. If you go too far in either direction, you are going to be unhappy and can't do much good for the world at large.

At one end of this spectrum of feeling lies *loneliness*. Everyone knows what that is. Loneliness is when you have no one to talk to and no one seems to care about you. If loneliness causes panic and drives you to merge with someone else, you may eventually experience the other extreme of distress: *engulfment*.

Loneliness seems easy to understand. There are songs and poetry written about it. Engulfment is more complicated. It is when your own identity seems to be swallowed up by other people's. Engulfment is when you perceive that you have no control over your life, that your independent sense of worth has been lost and that your personal needs have been sacrificed to those of others.

If you join a religious cult, your identity and independent judgment are going to be subverted as the leader tells you what to do and think. You are made to understand that your own needs and perceptions are worthless and that only the group matters. If your own identity is very weak, you may accept this control, but most of us are going to rebel. When we feel that someone is compromising our personal identity, we are going to pull away. We don't want to be engulfed.

The fear of engulfment is as terrifying in its own way as loneliness, and it can drive people to some extreme behavior, including hurting the people they love. In every romantic relationship there is a hidden war between loneliness and engulfment. When you are feeling lonely, you are drawn to be closer to your partner. When you feel swallowed up by them, you are driven to push them away. Most of the petty fights between romantic partners are unconscious reactions to perceived engulfment. When you are feeling overwhelmed or compromised by your partner or feel you have lost too much control to them, then you are going to pick a fight or do something else to create some distance between you.

This constant push and pull can be gentle or very violent. Hopefully, you can say, "I need my space right now," without your partner getting offended. Unfortunately, most people don't have that level of self-awareness and emotional control, and their cycle will be more extreme and theatrical. There will be frequent fights over trivial issues interspersed by equally superficial "making ups."

When volatile couples fight, they think they are fighting over whatever issue is in front of them. In fact, what really triggers the conflict is usually an emotional panic in one of the parties: "I can't breathe!" They feel that their identity is being drowned in the other, even if they can't put that feeling into words.

When marriages turn to hell, it is usually when one partner is feeling engulfed but doesn't have the means to regain their self-esteem or earn genuine identity on their own. Instead, they falsify an identity by generating conflict. Conflict gives the relationship the illusion of substance when one or both partners feel empty and lost in it.

The most volatile relationships tend to be those in which there is a gross imbalance of power. If one partner is much stronger in psychological or worldly terms, the weaker partner is going to feel engulfed and is likely to react with overt or covert aggression.

For example, imagine a rich and respected businessman who marries a young and beautiful "trophy wife" who has no real skills of her own. You would think the wife would be grateful, being that she has been "rescued" by this White Knight and has become as rich as he is without any effort. Turns out, though, they don't usually live happily ever after. The wife, feeling empty and useless, creates a pseudo-identity for herself by giving her husband hell. Every private sensation of "I am worthless" gets translated into "You are worthless," as she demands that her husband heal all the insecurities within her.

When White Knights swoop in to rescue Maidens in Distress, the fairy tales lead us to believe that they will both live happily ever after. Fat chance! The flipside of every rescue is a loss of control by the person being saved, which often emerges later as an engulfment reaction. Pretty soon, it is the knight who needs rescuing as the maiden badgers him over his perceived defects and creates conflicts where none previously existed.

In most cases, wise knights learn, the maiden must be left to rescue herself. Romantic relationships are successful, in the long term, only when power is relatively equal, when each person is responsible for their own problems and when a stable middle ground can be established between loneliness and engulfment.

For a healthy relationship, there have to be "boundaries." These are the borders beyond which you do not attempt to merge. You can fall in love and lose yourself in another person, but only up to a point. Where is that point? At what boundary line have you spent too much time with the one you love and have focused too much attention on them? You can't know this in advance. You have to figure it out dynamically by experimentation and negotiation.

Volatile relationships tend to swing violently from one passionate extreme to the other: First you are worshipping your partner, then reviling them. Stable relationships rely on more subtle adjustments: "I love you, but I need my space." For a relationship to be healthy, there have to be clear distinctions between my space, your space and our space. All of these boundaries need to be actively negotiated. They shouldn't all be mixed together in the same pot.

Love is not Charity

Romantic love is not a charity. It exists for your benefit, not your partner's.

Let me repeat that: The purpose of romantic love is to serve your own needs, not those of the person you love.

You are not a therapist. You are not a provider. You are not a parent. You are consumer. You should choose a romantic relationship solely because you believe it will give you good value for your investment. You can pay a reasonable price for the services received, but if the costs consistently exceed the benefits, or if you can clearly get better benefits elsewhere, then the relationship must end. Repeat: It must end! This may sound cold and selfish, but it's the only approach to love that's going to work in the long run.

Romantic love is not the same as parenthood, even if the attachment is similar. A parent is unconditionally responsible for their child. If your child is the Elephant Boy, hideous to the rest of the world, you don't love him any less. If your child is sick, you are going to care for him and try to get him the best medical attention. If your child behaves badly, you are going to be firm with him and do what you can to change the behavior, at least until he is an adult.

Responsible married people are tempted to apply this same standard of unconditional love to their spouse. After all, they said in their marriage vows, "For better or worse," and "In sickness and in health." If your partner gets arrested, you are going to stick by him. If your partner fails to do what he said he would, you give him another chance—and another and another. If he lapses into alcoholism, you try to get him into treatment. You know he had a deprived childhood, and you are willing to make accommodations for it. "I wouldn't abandon him if he got cancer," a distressed spouse may say, "so how can I leave him when he has a mental disorder?"

Unfortunately, this is a defective attitude that is bound to get you deeper into trouble. By attending unconditionally to your partner as though he were a child, you may be inadvertently "enabling" him and encouraging him to act like a child.

If your partner behaves badly, even once, there is really only one solution: withdrawal. If you aren't married, this isn't a big deal; you just go back to your natural independent position, living your own life and relying on your own resources. It may or may not be a permanent withdrawal, but your partner's psychological problems are simply not yours to solve.

There is a difference between a child and a grown adult. Children are still developing, whereas adults have reached a steady state that we on the outside have very little power to change. A small investment in a child can have substantial effects on their development, whereas a huge investment in an adult will probably have very little effect on their long-term personality.

A tragic childhood can help explain an adult's bad behavior, but it shouldn't change your response to it. If the behavior is noxious to you, you need to get away from it. Period.

Cooperative love between adults is completely different than a parent's love for a child. A parent's love exists mainly for the child's benefit. Romantic love is more of a business proposition, using criteria similar to what a business owner would use when hiring and firing an employee. If you can be bonded to only one partner at once, either this is going to be a competent employee, serving the needs of your business, or you should leave the position open for someone else.

This position is not a therapeutic one. You shouldn't hire someone because they are needy and you want to feel needed. You take them on only because you expect them to perform a service for you, just like any other employee. In the long term, the benefit to you has to be greater than the salary you are paying. You can make an ongoing investment in training, but you expect them to learn quickly. If the employee fails to perform to adequate standards within a reasonable time, you have to cut them loose.

What is their job description? You expect your partner to understand you, be interested in you and have enough language in common with you that you can freely talk to each other. They should speak not just English, but a functional dialect similar to yours. You expect to be able to share with them things that are important to you without fear of reprisal or indiscretion, and you expect to get intelligent and constructive feedback from them that is different than what you would tell yourself.

You don't need a sycophant or worshipper. You are looking for a confidential observer who sees the world through different eyes and who can give you important new data about yourself and your problems. It is a lot like a president hiring an advisor. The advisor, knowing the president well, can give him an honest assessment of his own policies when no one else can.

What is the price of this arrangement? You have to be willing to do the same for the other person.

Sex can be included in this business arrangement, but it is not really the purpose of it. There should be tenderness and intimacy, because the closer you are to each other, the better you can communicate. Mutual aid can be part of the agreement. When your employee is facing unexpected personal problems, you can do what you can to help, within reasonable boundaries. You are willing to invest a large portion of your time and resources in this employee, because you know how valuable they will be to you in the long run.

If they fail to perform their duties, however, they're out! A president wouldn't accept an advisor who came to work drunk. Correction: A president *may* accept an advisor who came to work drunk, because they have no doubt known each other for years and are familiar with each other's weaknesses. What the president could not accept is defective information from the advisor. If the advisor wasn't really advising and wasn't providing honest and reliable information when it was needed, then he would have to be replaced with another.

If you find yourself repeatedly digging your employee out of his own problems, you probably don't need them. Whether you keep them on the payroll comes down to a cold, hard calculation of whether the salary you are paying is worth the information you are getting.

It is not immoral to invest in a relationship for the practical ongoing benefit you are getting out of it. Remember that this is your only opportunity for this level of intimacy. It is not like a parent who can raise six kids at once. Because of the huge investment involved, you can probably have only one intimate advisor at a time, so your standards need to be high. If you aren't getting adequate return on your investment, then it is better to be alone and leave the position unfilled.

If you want to treat alcoholism, give to the Salvation Army. If you want to devote yourself to helping others, then focus on those who can most realistically be changed—using whatever *extra* resources you have at your disposal after you have provided for your own needs. Your one special position must be exempt from all charity: It must *not* be used as an avenue for directly helping someone. An intimate relationship can be therapeutic for both parties, but this is incidental. The real purpose of the relationship is to give you advice and counsel you can't get elsewhere.

What happens if your partner gets sick—physically sick—and can't perform the duties required? Let's say they contract Alzheimer's Disease or some other wasting illness beyond their control. Would you abandon them because they aren't performing their job? Probably not. You would then revert to a parental role, in part to repay them for their past service, but then your special position would be open again.

A bona fide illness does not include personality disorders. This is your partner's self-destructiveness due to some defect in their childhood. These diseases are untreatable by medical means and probably untreatable even by psychotherapy. The subject remains physically sound, just self-destructive and perhaps abusive of you. If that is the case, the only thing you can do is cut them loose because they aren't performing the job and because anything you do will only enable them.

If the employee isn't doing their job, therapy is beyond your abilities. For the sake of your mission, you need to fill the position with someone more competent. Forget about "For better or worse." You've got a business to run!

The Dilemma of Beauty

Young romantics dream of bonding with their partner for life, but the way medical science is progressing "life" could be over 100 years by the time they get there! The direction of current technology suggests you will spend your final years as a brain in jar connected by wires to the internet. Your partner will presumably occupy the jar beside you. There will be a high capacity coaxial connection directly between the two jars so you can nag and annoy each other more efficiently. At that point, your bodies will become irrelevant. All that will matter will be your minds and the special language you have built together.

That's pretty much the way things already are! Once you have lived with someone for a while, you don't see their body anymore. They are essentially a gender-less brain in the jar beside you who you are communicating with through a special high-bandwidth connection. Hopefully, your communication gets more subtle with time, to the point where it is almost telepathic. At the same time, you should each be maintaining your own independent relationship with the rest of the world, so you actually have something to communicate about when you come together.

Even if sexual attraction brought you together, it is destined to fade into the background, and it is not what keeps you coming back to each other. All that matters in the long run is the quality and usefulness of your communication. Your relationship will succeed or fail based on it.

If sex is ultimately irrelevant, a logical question is whether sexual attraction is really the best criteria for choosing your mate to begin with. It's an awkward thought. If the most important thing is talent, can that talent be enclosed in a physical package you find sexually unappealing? If the physical attraction isn't there, but everything else is, should you close your eyes and dive in anyway? Is it acceptable to fall in love with someone for their perceived physical beauty? Does beauty count, or is it only a distraction?

People have no choice about the basic body they were born into, which is determined by their genes. However, also programmed by our genes are certain innate standards of beauty that even infants recognize. An objectively beautiful man or woman, as perceived by other humans, has facial features and body parts in the right proportions. If someone's eyes are too far apart or too close together, it clashes with the image of beauty that our brain is programmed with. A person has absolutely no control over the spacing of their eyes, so is it fair to judge them by it?

For that matter, is it fair to discriminate based on *any* physical characteristic—age, height, weight, gender? If a woman will date only men who are taller than her, isn't she eliminating a significant portion of the talent pool? Can't a short man be just as good a communicator? For that matter, why do you have to limit yourself to a single gender? If you are a man who is sexually attracted to women but another man comes along who meets all your other criteria, is it fair to "discriminate" against him solely because of his gender?

It's a touchy subject no one likes to think about. No one wants to discriminate, but the fact remains that you are attracted to some physical specimens and not others. Are you a sexist, heightist, weightist, ageist bigot? Knowing that physical characteristics are going to fade into the background anyway, how do you reconcile your sexual preferences with the illogic of it all?

First, let's emphasize again: Love is not charity. You should never, *ever* fall in love with someone because you pity them, feel sorry for them or want to help them. Remember you are engaging in love primarily to serve your own needs, not the other person's. (Of course, you also expect to pay a reasonable price for this service.) You also expect them to come up to speed on your needs relatively fast. You don't want to have to invest months or years in training without reward; things should "click" from an early stage.

You also have to recognize that physical beauty can mask a lot of ugly things. A beautiful woman or handsome guy, defined by biological standards, can still be an asshole once you start living with them. In fact, *too much* objective beauty can be a warning sign. When someone is beautiful and everyone knows it, they are tempted to skate by on their looks alone and are less likely to seek deeper kinds of accomplishment. Do you really want to be dating the homecoming queen or the class stud? Do you expect much depth between the ears?

The pool of competent potential partners will always be limited, so you have to be open to a broad range of physical specimens: young/old, tall/short, svelte/beefy. But at what point does their weight tip the scales into ugly obesity? Should a midget be dating a basketball star? Should you be considering someone with a good mind who you are only marginally attracted to? Remember that you are both going to end up in jars anyway.

To answer the question, we have to step back a bit. Remember that sex itself is pretty loony. Logically, our body shape shouldn't make any difference at all in our relations with others, but it does in the sexual arena. Over time, sex is going to be less and less relevant to a relationship, but it may be important for getting it started.

Sex can be thought of as a tool—like a can opener—to help us get started at intimacy. It can help us overcome the substantial natural barriers between individuals. Without sex, you might not achieve the level of intimacy necessary to start the special communication going.

Romantic intimacy is like nuclear fusion. You need a lot of energy to get the reaction started, but after a certain break-even point, the process is self-sustaining. Sexual attraction can provide that initial energy source.

If that's what you are using sex for, then your innate sexual preferences must be factored in. Whatever turns you on has to be listened to—as long as it doesn't get too kinky. The fact that you are attracted to one body type and not another may not make a lot of logical sense, but if you ignore these feelings, then you'll be faking it, and you won't get very far in the intimacy game.

There are also many components of beauty that each person has a huge amount of control over, like one's carriage and self-maintenance. You may have little control over the bone structure you have been given, but you have great control over how you present it and take care of it. It is like the difference between a clean, well-maintained car and a dirty, broken-down one that the owner obviously takes no pride in. The car itself may be a standard model, but its maintenance and presentation reflects the owner's personality.

If love is not charity, then you are looking for talent, and talent itself can be beautiful. Even someone who you would not judge as striking in a photograph can be incredibly appealing in person. Once animated, the appearance of the face and body is less genetic than a reflection of a person's chosen values.

The characteristics of beauty that one has reasonable control over are fair criteria for romantic judgment. You should care that someone takes pride in their appearance, even if they are no god or goddess. The color or texture of a person's skin is less important than them being comfortable in it. Self-confidence has its outer presentation. It we are sensitive to the right cues, they might lead us toward the right person, even if we all end up in jars in the end.

The Problems of Communism

"From each according to his abilities, to each according to his needs."

That's the Communist credo. In a perfect society, people who are strong should use their surplus resources to take care of those who are weak. Communism was supposed to address the huge disparities between wealth and poverty that still exist today. It is obscene to see how some people ostentatiously waste money while others a short distance away are struggling just to make ends meet.

Marriage is Communism in miniature, involving only two people instead of a whole society. You are choosing to combine all your income and expenses in one pot and share from it according to need. When you make your vows and enter into the legal contract of marriage, you think that everything is going to be equal between you from this day forward. You will do what you are good at and your spouse will do what they are good at, and together you will get everything done. Each of you will work just as hard as the other and with equal quality. In the evening, you will collapse into each other's arms, happy with your day's labor and content in your Worker's Paradise.

What is wrong with this ideal arrangement? Pretty much the same things that brought down Communism in the late 20th Century. Communism tried to equalize things by taking from the rich and giving to the poor. In the process, it destroyed the incentive for quality. If you receive no reward for exceptional performance, then you probably aren't going to attempt it. In fact, if you do more than is expected of you, Communism will penalize you for it, because your quota will be raised and the system will continue to expect this level of output from you in the future. Furthermore, if you are protected from the consequences of your mistakes, you are less inclined to correct them.

No matter how well intentioned it may have been, Communism only reduced the total pool of resources and enforced bland mediocrity. Over time, some people become "more equal" than others. Some shouldered more of the work while others who could get away with it did less. The whole society became less productive.

In marital communism, you run the same principle risk: One person ends up doing more of the productive work of the relationship while the other does progressively less and net productivity falls. If you start out your marriage with a gung-ho attitude, eagerly giving more than you get, your partner will probably adjust to that and this elevated quota will be expected of you permanently. If you wash the dishes during your honeymoon, pretty soon you find yourself washing them every night. If you make accommodations for your partner's weaknesses and sensitivities, soon even more accommodations will be expected of you.

Everyone has fears—personal challenges they don't want to face and bad habits they are reluctant to give up. If you give people the option of letting someone else shoulder the responsibility for those fears, they'll take it! It is only human nature. The creation of a common pot, in a society of two or two million, gives individuals the temptation of relying on the pot whenever their fear level rises and the going gets tough. If the pot is doled out generously, people will draw from it generously to avoid their own responsibility.

What this usually means in a marriage is that if one person

does a little more work or takes a little more responsibility, the other will accept it and expect it. Over time, this makes one party stronger and more serving and the other progressively weaker and more demanding.

The alternative economic system, Capitalism, is more rational but not much prettier. "What's mine is mine and yours is yours." Each person is strictly accountable for their performance regardless of their circumstances. If you get sick, lose a leg or happen to be a child, that's your problem. Capitalism won't take care of you.

If you engage in any romantic relationship, you are agreeing to abandon some aspects of Capitalism. To be in love, you must be willing to share things with your partner without a strict accounting of who contributes what. Mutual aid is also part of the deal: If something bad happens to your partner, you will be there to help them. To get the most from life, you have to be willing to share at least some of yourself in a communistic way. The question is, at what point does sharing become destructive and counterproductive?

Without marriage and its draconian financial merger, the two of you would have to actively negotiate how you share. Maybe you decide to split the rent, utilities and other household expenses 50-50. Whatever money you each have left is yours alone, and you are each free to spend your own surplus as you wish without consulting the other. If you see something expensive you want, and you have money in your pocket, you are free to buy it, no permission or negotiation required, because that money is yours.

If you throw everything into a common pot, then you have to negotiate everything. If nothing else, this can be extremely burdensome and bureaucratic. You can't go out and buy anything you want with your own money, because "your own money" doesn't exist. You have to clear it with your spouse. No matter how much two people may love each other, they are bound to have different goals and visions for their income. It may make sense to pool rent and household expenses into a common pot, but not everything else.

Because the new pot is bigger and more complex than an individual's finances, each person is less connected to the consequences of their actions. What this means in many marriages is an explosion of debt! Because no one person is clearly responsible for creating the debt or reining it in, responsibility is diluted and confused. Because the common pot has more available credit than each individual, consequences may be delayed. By the time both parties recognize there is a cash flow problem, it may already be catastrophic.

"Two can live as cheaply as one," is usually a myth. In reality, couples may spend more extravagantly than single people because the community as a whole is only as disciplined as its least disciplined partner. Communities are also less innovative and creative in finding cheaper solutions to their problems. It is the bureaucratic factor. To do something differently, you need consultation and permission. If you are willing to make a financial compromise but your spouse isn't, you'll probably stick with the more expensive solution by default. If you were alone, you would just decide what needs to be done and do it!

Marriages, like Communist states, always start out with high ideals: We are going to share everything equally! Unfortunately, true equality can be incredibly difficult to maintain in a communistic environment. It is like two stars orbiting close to each other. Inherently, the system is unstable. Even if they start out equally, eventually one is going to start sucking more material out of the other than it is giving back.

In a marriage, however, it is not usually the stronger party who is sucking resources out of the weaker but the other way around. As one party gains in strength, the other tends to get more emotional, throw more tantrums and demand more attention. As the weaker party feels increasingly useless, they compensate by magnifying their discomforts and generating artificial conflicts.

It is amusing to watch this dynamic in gay couples. With uncanny regularity, the couple evolves into a strong "provider", who goes out and competently deals with the world, and a more emotional "housewife" who overreacts to everything and requires constant attention. The hysterical wife remains perpetually needy because the provider is willing to provide. Receiving more than he produces paradoxically suppresses the self-esteem of the needy one, who may be tempted to create disruptions to try to reassert his identity. The substance of the relationship often consists of a series of repetitive sitcom scenarios where the needy one creates problems and the more competent one dutifully comes along to clean up the mess.

Think of Homer and Marge Simpson. Isn't Marge an enabler? Doesn't her strength and willingness to clean up Homer's messes ultimately encourage his oafishness? Now, think of marriages in the town where you grew up—say, the parents of your friends who you were able to watch at close range. In how many of those marriages was power truly equal? Wasn't one partner usually more dependent and child-like, taking more than they gave?

By throwing all your finances into one collective pot, you are erasing healthy boundaries and destroying natural incentives. The result may be a system of perverse incentives that encourage irresponsible behavior. When the going gets tough and there is a secure safety net beneath you, it is easy to fall back on it rather than facing unpleasant choices and changes of habit. Any system of protection can encourage this unhealthy dependency. One party stops standing up for themselves because they no longer have to, while the one with ability feels obligated to pick up the slack.

The presence of this dysfunctional dynamic does not necessarily mean the marriage will collapse. There are many kinds of marriage hell that do not end. In the Soviet Union, Communism cranked along in dull matrimony for 70 years. If there are enough natural resources available, a communist society can be sustained for a lifetime. It is just not a healthy society.

Stagnation or regression wasn't what you hoped for when you started your revolution, was it?

The Dark Star Duet

There can be many reasons why marriages end in divorce, but one model seems common in Family Court. I call it the "Dark Star Duet."

Imagine a binary star system: two stars revolving closely around each other. One star is normal like our sun, and the other is a black hole. The black hole sucks up more energy than it gives, so the normal star must give out more than it gets. A continuous stream of matter and energy is drawn from the healthy star to the black hole, never to be seen again.

This is the perfect model for how many marriages work. One party is the provider, perhaps too strong and adaptive for his or her own good, and the other is the perpetual child: needy, jealous, demanding and increasingly unstable.

This model knows no sexual preference. It happens in gay relationships and straight ones, legal marriages or ad hoc ones. "He" or "she" could be either party, so I will just call them "Light" and "Dark" using the masculine gender for both. Here is the usual scenario...

There have always been substantial differences between Light and Dark. Light is the responsible one, the flexible one, the one who can rise to any challenge. Dark is insecure one, the inflexible one, the one who freaks out at any unexpected change and who always needs a crutch to lean on. In a way, they were made for each other. Dark was needy, and Light was willing to give.

Looking back on the relationship after the divorce, you can usually say that the warning signs were always there, but Light chose to sweep them under the carpet. From the beginning, Light could see some of Dark's helplessness, but it seemed endearing at the time. Helping Dark made Light feel loved and useful. Dark was grateful at first and didn't complain. He was troubled, but not abusive.

Dark's insecurities seemed like nothing Light's love couldn't fix. It turned out, however, that a secure relationship only made matters worse. Confident that Light wouldn't leave, Dark took more and more from him and stopped appreciating what he did. The more Dark took, the more he became unstable and abusive. Light felt less loved and more like a servant. He felt like he was walking on eggshells, carefully watching everything he said and did to avoid setting off Dark's anger.

That's the scary side of security. Whenever you have a communistic system where people are supposed to share everything equally, one party often starts taking too much while the other must give more than his fair share to make up for it. The funny thing is, the more the weaker party draws from the common pot, the more angry and complaining he becomes. That's because his self-esteem is draining away at the same time and he needs to compensate with more distracting theatrics. If he doesn't have a real identity, he creates the illusion of it by generating problems to get the other's attention.

If Dark faces a painful decision in the real world but has the easy backup plan of obtaining the artificial protection of Light, he's usually going to take advantage of it, expecting Light's rescue. Light, being ever-adaptable, is usually willing to play the rescuer, especially to avoid Dark's abusive behavior. What neither seems to see is that each rescue is just making the system more unstable.

Dark's behavior gets worse and worse! The more he relies

on Light, the more Dark's self-esteem plummets because he has done nothing to earn it. The loss of self-esteem leads to panic whenever Dark is forced to face the outside world alone or when Light seems to be pulling away. Panic, in turn, leads to more bad behavior. Soon, Dark can't politely ask for Light's help, which would be too humiliating. He has to manipulate Light through temper tantrums, vague health complaints, alcohol and drug use, passive-aggressive obstruction and other forms of face-saving trickery.

This bad behavior may not have been present before the marriage, when Dark was reasonably independent and functional, facing the world on his own. Marriage created the dys-function! Dark believes that marriage means his partner will take care of everything, especially when he is feeling uncomfortable or unwell—which is now most of the time. As time goes on, Dark's complaints grow in number and intensity while Light rushes around trying to address them. Because their fates are now merged, Light is always willing to pick up the slack to keep the peace, which essentially gives Dark permission to be even more ill and dysfunctional.

Soon the binary model becomes obvious: the dark star is sucking energy out of the light one and giving little in return. You might think this would automatically result in divorce, as Light gets tired of covering for Dark all the time, but it usually doesn't. It's a duet, remember! Light feels responsible for Dark's dysfunction and recalls his promise to stick by his partner "in sickness and in health." As Dark becomes more "sick" and detached from outside reality, Light feels he can't withdraw because "Dark would never survive without me."

It's the perfect dance of Yin and Yang, addict and enabler, black hole and entrapped star, and it will usually continue as long as sufficient outside resources are available to support the system. If Light is a good provider and the bills are getting paid, the dysfunctional duet will probably go on and on. Being true to his word ("In sickness and in health"), Light usually isn't willing to make the break unless the dysfunction gets so bad he has no choice. He is as addicted to the dysfunction as Dark is! Especially if there are children involved, the costs of divorce just seem too high, so Light tries to survive through appeasement, overcompensation and denial.

Marriages like this can limp along for years, and they are all around us if we care to look. The absence of divorce in these cases is a tragedy for everyone, because Dark would actually do better on his own. He needs to face the real world directly without the artificial and ultimately debilitating protection of Light. Unfortunately, neither Dark nor Light will withdraw gracefully. Both have to be pushed.

If the mutual dysfunction exceeds the outside resources to support it, the system will eventually collapse. Divorce *will* happen, but can take a long time to get there, sometimes years or decades after the disease becomes obvious. It would be healthier for everyone if it happened sooner, at the first indication of trouble, but it is human nature to hold on… and on and on!

I can't tell you how to escape, but I can tell you counseling isn't going to help. Negotiating from a handcuffed position won't help. There's no talking it out, because Dark's whole personality is the issue and the relationship itself is exacerbating the problem. You either take action by stepping out of this star system or you don't, letting the dysfunction continue to fester.

'Til death do you part.

A Bureaucracy of Two

One is the loneliest number. It is also the most efficient, flexible and creative number. The vast majority of mankind's most important artistic works, from books and movies to great scientific ideas, were the product of one. Others may have helped, but only one had the vision and control. Committees can't write great books, paint great paintings or lead armies in times of war. When you are challenging the creative limits of anything, only an individual has the internal coherence to pull it off.

Couples and other kinds of teams can have great accomplishments together, but these are usually "second wave" expeditions after one person alone blazed the trail. Teams, by and large, don't blaze trails; they can only support and follow the one individual who does. This is the reason most business organizations have only one ultimate leader, not two. It simply works better that way. The leader can consult with others and call upon a team for advice and support, but the fundamental decision-making unit has to be one person alone.

The problem with two is deciding who will be responsible for what. If two people become CEO of a corporation, how will they divide up the tasks between them? Who will the staff go to when there is a problem? Equal cooperation may work when the decisions are easy, but when the ship starts taking on water, you've got to have real leadership, which doesn't come in twos. If one general isn't put clearly in charge of an army, with the courage and power to make painful decisions, it cannot expect to win a war.

One is a necessary number, because one person can hold in their head more subtle ideas, plans and compromises than can possibly be worked out between multiple people. In a crisis, only one person can weigh a lot of complicated and conflicting factors and respond in real time with one optimal solution. Only one person can effectively assert authority and convey a consistent position to their subordinates. Only one person can step outside the box and rethink a problem in a totally new way.

The alternative form of leadership is a committee. Committees can get things done only when the goals of the group are simple and stable and can be conveyed between members in words. For a collective management to work effectively, the destination and the means to reach it have to be clearly defined. If you instruct a committee to build a skyscraper according to the plans you provide, they can hire and coordinate the many contractors and thousands of workers to get the job done. The one thing a committee can't do is produce those original plans.

In a romantic relationship, the two of you form a committee. No matter how in sync you seem to be, the two of you together are unlikely to produce decisions that are as subtle, competent or creative as one person potentially can. In any complex project, one person can certainly assist the other, contributing their independent judgment and supportive labor, but one leader alone has to be in charge.

A couple in love can probably be trusted to put together a jigsaw puzzle together, dividing up the work in cooperative ways. That's the sort of well-defined, ritualized, labor-intensive task a team is good at. A couple can't be trusted to *create* the puzzle, however. That's one person's job.

Two is supposed to be the optimal number for raising children, but is it really? If a child needs permission for something and Mom denies it, what is he going to do? Go to Dad, of course! If the two parents are inconsistent, as they inevitably are, then the child can choose whichever answer he prefers. In the myth of perfect equality, the parents are in perfect harmony and reinforce each other's decisions. In reality, there is usually a substantial gap between the two and they erode each other's discipline and authority.

Love works only when each partner knows when to defer to the other's leadership, without becoming needy and dependent. If the two of you go into the kitchen together intending to create a great gourmet meal, there can be only one head chef. He tells the sous-chef what to do, and no matter how skilled the sous-chef may be in his own right, he has to be willing to take the back seat and follow the other's lead. There can be no greater disaster than two celebrity chefs going into a kitchen on equal terms and trying to create a single meal. It just doesn't work.

The potential benefit of a relationship is that your partner can give you independent feedback and thereby enhance the quality of your own leadership decision-making. The possible risk, however, is that a relationship will "dumb down" your decision making. If you are forced to seek consensus with your partner on things that you can better handle alone, then you may have to settle for clumsy solutions you both agree on but that you know aren't the best.

Committees tend to make poor decisions under stress and during periods of rapid change. No one is willing to make the hard, politically-incorrect choices to get the organization out of whatever mess it is in. Committees don't like to lay off staff, accept strategic losses or kill anybody's pet project. Committees want only happy solutions.

Likewise, when a married couple faces a crisis together, the need for consensus may prevent the team from making the unthinkable decisions to solve the crisis. The wiser party may say, "We have no choice, we have to sell the house," but if their partner doesn't agree, then no action will be taken. Ideally, in a crisis, you want to move quickly, but a bureaucracy never moves quickly. As hard as it may be for one person to make a decision under stress, the more difficult challenge may be convincing their partner to go along. If the partner can't be recruited for the plan, then the status quo prevails, and they will both sink together.

In the dysfunctional norm, a marriage turns into a bureaucracy of two where you are forced to seek permission for every decision you make. You can't move a piece of furniture without filling out Form XJ-17A and having it signed by your partner. If you fail to get permission, and somebody's toes get stepped on, you know there will be hell to pay.

In the beginning of the relationship—the falling in love phase—everything your partner does is "no problem." They are just so wonderful in your eyes that they can do no wrong. After a while, however, territoriality sets in. Your partner cuts down your favorite rose bush, and you start demanding they consult with you before doing such things. That's when the bureaucracy begins.

A single person, rummaging through his closet (or his life), can easily say, "I don't need this anymore. I'm throwing it out." Don't try that when you are married! Throwing out anything requires Form GB-137c, signed, sealed and notarized in triplicate. This applies not just to unused objects but also to time-consuming activities that no longer serve a purpose. The ship has to actually be sinking, the band playing "Nearer My God to Thee," before some passengers are willing to jettison their baggage.

All relationships demand a certain degree of mutual accountability. Even if you aren't married to the person you are living with, you want to know when they'll be home at night. This accountability can be warm and gentle, but it can still be a burden on your creativity. The more you need to seek permission for things, the less capable you are of implementing complex, rapid and inspired solutions that only you understand.

In the simple projects that two people choose to share, the status quo is usually the preferred option. They go back to the same restaurants they have been to before and repeat the same sentimental activities. The management of the household proceeds on automatic: Once your home has been set up, things tend to stay the same for long periods. Within a relationship, there aren't usually a lot of radical changes. When you find patterns you both feel comfortable with and that cause the least conflict, you tend to stick with them.

It is an unfortunate fact of life that long-term emotional relationships tend to inhibit change, creativity, personal growth and dynamic movement in new directions. Relationships require consistency and don't flourish in conditions of uncertainty. This is one of the trade-offs of love that you have to live with.

If you want to be a secret agent, licensed to kill, roaming the world in Her Majesty's Secret Service, then you probably have to remain unattached. In this kind of creative position, you need to be able to change course instantly to serve your mission, and you can't be putting your partner through the wringer every time you go to work. You can't be calling up all the time, "Dear, I'm in Singapore about to be sliced in two by a laser. I'm going to be late for dinner." Real relationships won't tolerate that kind of uncertainty.

If you are unattached, you probably want to fall in love, but once you do, it is bound to slow down at least some aspects of your own personal development. For one thing, a relationship occupies a lot of time, taking you away from your own developmental projects. Secondly, your partner is going to embody a certain worldview, which in turn will probably lock you into a limited conceptual neighborhood.

Imagine you are a police detective and you fall in love with another police detective who you meet at work. You have a common language together (filled with acronyms and code names) and can talk about your jobs with great subtlety and ease. The one thing that becomes more difficult, however, is switching careers. Becoming bonded to someone who shares your interests may seem admirable, but it also tends to have a reinforcing effect, binding you to that lifestyle and culture.

After bonding with a fellow police detective, you are less likely to wake up tomorrow and decide you want to be, say, a teacher in Alaska. To make changes like this, you may have to leave your partner behind, at least in the sense that you may lose your shared language and your common experience. This kind of radical and inspired change is relatively painless for a single person but is inherently stressful in a relationship, so it doesn't happen often.

Before you fall in love and certainly before you marry, consider this: To a significant degree, any relationship is going to freeze you at whatever developmental stage you were in when the bonding occurred. If you marry your high school sweetheart, your development is going to be frozen at the high school level and not grow too far beyond it.

You probably know former high school classmates like that: those who found romantic "success" at an early stage and were nailed in place by it. They never left your hometown! They're still working at the local factory, and if you go back to visit them, you may see that their bodies have aged but their brains haven't changed much. From your point of view, they stepped into a time capsule at graduation and never left.

This is a dangerous effect of romance, especially when followed by marriage, debt and children. You think that love is going to open up new worlds to you, but instead it shuts them down.

Commercial Delusions

A love interest seems to be required in every mainstream Hollywood movie. Not only must the hero fight the terrorists to save the world, he also has to win the girl. There are car chases and gun battles, and at some point it seems that both the world and the girl are lost. Then, at the last minute, just as the clock on the bomb ticks down to zero, the hero rallies his strength, defeats the enemy and saves the girl. They fall into each others' arms. The End.

What the movies never seem to show us is what happens next. What are the man and woman supposed to do now that they have found each other? If the movie shows anything at all of their future relationship, it is a wedding, with all the supporting cast present. The wedding proves symbolically that the relationship is a "success" and that all the problems between them have been resolved.

While there are countless movies about finding love, there are few about how to conduct a relationship. There simply isn't enough drama in it. Routine married life is portrayed to the public primarily in television commercials. In the space of 30 seconds, we meet a man and woman in a prototypical suburban home. They have a problem, which will eventually be solved by the advertised product. The purpose of the commercial, of course, is to sell the product, but first it has to create the fantasy of the perfect life that the product will fit into.

Imagine if you were an alien—or a human—whose

only information about life on Earth came from television commercials. It would be a curious and very restricted picture. On Earth, the commercials show us, every family lives in a spacious two-story single-family house in a green and leafy neighborhood. The couple who lives in the house is a man and woman of the same race and about the same age. The woman is slightly smaller than the man, and neither of them is overweight. They are attractive but not glamorous. Their interaction indicates an easy confidence in each other. There may be deception between them, but it is always benign. For example, if the wife serves dinner rolls to her husband and he thinks they're homemade, she might not reveal they are store-bought. Only the viewer knows.

Their only distress concerns the problem solved by the product. "Honey," says one, sitting with a calculator and a pile of papers on the kitchen table, "I don't think we can retire as soon as we planned." That sets up the scenario for the product to be introduced. Most TV ads unfold the same way. First, an idealized environment is created: the perfect American home. Then, a problem is introduced and is briefly explained. Finally, the product is brought in to solve the problem. Look, no more greasy build-up!

It is all staged, of course. The house doesn't exist but is simulated in a studio. The husband and wife are actors who probably don't even know each other. Their dilemma is orchestrated in such a way that the product perfectly solves it. Obviously, the whole production was paid for by the company that is selling the product and that wants to sell more. Viewers know this, at least on an intellectual level, but on an emotional level, the charade still works. People who have seen the commercial and who identify with the characters are more likely to buy the product.

The incidental product these commercials are selling is a fantasy image of marriage and family life. These families aren't chaotic. Their homes are perfectly clean. Everyone knows their role. There aren't any conflicts except humorous ones, and every problem can be solved by buying a product.

Advertising sends a subliminal message to the public that the normal mode of life is married, with children, living in a spacious suburban house. It isn't the only possible lifestyle in the real world, but it is one most often portrayed in commercials. Why this particular lifestyle? Because it sells more products! Advertisers want you to sign on to this fantasy of the American Dream, because then they can sell you the accessories to that dream. They can't sell you furniture if you don't have a place to put it, and they can't sell you jewelry if you don't have a spouse or fiancé to give it to.

Think about jewelry commercials. What are they selling? Jewelry! But they are also selling an idealized vision of marital love that facilitates jewelry sales. How do you show your wife that you care? You buy her a diamond, and she'll love you for it.

Isn't this a sick relationship message? If you want more love from your partner, you bribe them! The insidious effect of modern advertising is it encourages people to try to buy themselves out of relationship problems. Flowers, chocolate and Hallmark cards are never going to repair underlying problems of communication, but the commercial world wants you to believe that they can.

If you are married and you buy your spouse a diamond, you are paying for it out of the community pot, so your spouse is really paying for half of it. In a sense, it isn't really a gift at all. It's like stealing from your roommate to give him a birthday present!

People enter into marriage with an idealized image of what it should be. Part of that image comes from watching real married couples, such as one's own parents and neighbors, who might not be revealing everything. The other part comes from mass media. Commercial media, unfortunately, always has something to promote and is not going to tell you everything either. It has one overriding goal: to sell products.

Romantic relationships require a complex set of methods and skills, like sailing a ship. There aren't really any products that can help you learn these skills. Even relationship books don't help much. You just have to get out there and start sailing, then be smart enough to learn from your misadventures.

Media is not your friend in this regard. It is bound to fill your head with distracting ideas that only slow down the learning process. You don't need 99.9% of the things media is selling you. There are things in life you do need, but advertising isn't going to lead you to them because they aren't profitable.

Media portrays a standardized world of cookie-cutter roles. You don't need that. You just need pragmatic ways to solve your own unique problems. First, you figure out what your problems are, then you experiment with ways to address them, which usually have nothing to do with a purchased product. Your solution can be a unique one that works only for you, that you can't explain to anyone else and that doesn't make anyone else any money.

If a relationship works, in private, between the two of you, that's all you can ask of it. How it looks from the outside shouldn't matter. If you start conforming to public models, then you are inevitably giving up something in the private quality of your relationship.

Which will it be? Are you going to play a role for an outside audience, or build the best working relationship that you can?

Wedding Pornography

Something deeply ingrained in the human brain and genome draws men to pornography. Even on the flat printed page, seeing the naked female form or the crude sex act seems to trigger male pleasure circuits—almost as much, it seems, as real three-dimensional females and actual cooperative intercourse.

In the second half of the 20th Century, this pornographic urge fueled a huge publishing industry. Glossy mainstream magazines like *Playboy* portrayed the idealized female figure in seductive poses, while countless grittier and lesser-known publications briefed the male on feminine gynecology and the objects that could be inserted therein.

Attempts to develop similar pornography for woman never really took off. There was a magazine called *Playgirl* that depicted naked men in sensual poses, but this turned out to be of greater interest to gay males than it did to genetic females. Females don't seem to respond as strongly to that kind of visual stimuli. That's not to say that they aren't genetically programmed to respond to pornography or that a vast and useless industry can't be built upon this urge. It's just a different kind of pornography.

In the early 21st Century, video pornography on the internet decimated the printed pornography industry, at least for the male market. *Playboy*, once a half-inch thick with lucrative advertising, became only a thin shadow of itself. Printed pornography for woman, however, remained as lucrative and shameless as ever. You still see it in public places: Young women drooling unabashedly over their thick and glossy magazines, thinking selfish and erotic thoughts. These magazines don't depict naked men. Instead they show beautiful women in idealized poses... often dressed in wedding gowns!

Some of the most popular female pornography, at least judging by magazine sales, seems to be focused on the wedding ceremony. You can call me sexist, but when have you seen a thick and glossy wedding magazine targeted at men? Just like sex porn seems to be a male addiction, wedding porn seems to be primarily a female one.

The male himself is little more than an accessory in this process. His only duties are to show up at the ceremony, wear the standard tuxedo assigned to him and say "I do" when instructed. It is the bride, her female relatives and her girlfriends who get all hot and bothered about a wedding, usually for months and sometimes years preceding it. The male is dutifully "consulted" in the planning stages, but it is rarely more than a pro forma consultation. His primary duty is to say "Yes" and sign whatever piece of paper is stuck under his nose. There is little doubt who is in charge of this operation.

Weddings come in two kinds: fast or extravagant. Here in Las Vegas, we specialize in the fast variety. You meet someone special and feel, based on three weeks of experience, that this is the perfect match, so you run off to Vegas to tie the knot—quick, before you change your mind! The aim here is to escape the usual ponderous wedding machinery (and the usual safeguards) and just do it. In Las Vegas, we can get you married in under two hours, with a variety of available wedding packages that may include flowers, organ music, a video of the event and ministry by Elvis.

If you don't take the Vegas route, then you are condemned to include all of your friends and relatives in the ceremony, and the event will quickly balloon into a massive monster with a life of its own. Especially if this is your first wedding, things can't be done simply. For one thing, you don't think of it as your "first" wedding. You believe this will be your "only" wedding, so you think you need to pull out all the stops.

The wedding procedures are strictly programmed by perceived tradition and commercial marketing. Couples often try to deviate from these procedures to make their event seem unique (e.g. getting married on a mountaintop), but they are still defined by the traditions. In a Christian-based ceremony, there will probably be bridesmaids and a best man, who will carry the ring. There will be wedding cake, which has to be eaten by the bride and groom in a certain way. The guests will have to be fed, usually at the expense of the couple and their families, and a photographer must be hired to record the event. The bride will throw her bouquet into a crowd of unmarried woman. At the end, the couple will drive off in a car with "Just Married" embarrassingly displayed on the windows.

In practical terms, we're talking about a huge expenditure in both planning and money. $10,000 might get you by in America, but don't count on it! A good rule of thumb is that an average wedding and honeymoon will absorb whatever money you have in the bank plus the current limit on your credit cards.

What is the purpose of a wedding? We already know that, under the law, marriage is little more than an economic contract to share future assets and liabilities. Nowadays in America, people can comfortably live together, buy property and raise children without marriage, so there isn't anything you can do after the wedding that you couldn't do before. How does a complicated wedding ceremony change anything? Why do people feel that they need the extravagant public event when a simple trip to the courthouse or Las Vegas will do?

Intellectually, couples usually say that the wedding isn't

going to change their relationship. They love each other before the ceremony and will love each other no less or more after it. So why do they need the ceremony at all? Obviously, people wouldn't engage in such an expensive project if they didn't expect it to change something. If it isn't going to change the couple themselves, is it supposed to change their family and friends?

A wedding ceremony seems to be a form of advertising. It is a loud announcement to the world that a change is happening: John and Sue, once single people, are now man and wife. What is accomplished by making this announcement? Maybe it is a declaration to your family and friends that you have finally "grown up." It could be a sort of coming-of-age ceremony, where you claim to the world that the insecurities of childhood are over and you have finally arrived at solid, stable adulthood.

But the wedding ceremony could also have another purpose. It could be a sort of magical talisman that is supposed to give the relationship substance and certainty when you are feeling privately ambivalent about it. Although rational people may claim to not believe in magic, that is exactly what the betrothed are looking for.

The first President Bush—who turned out in retrospect to be the wiser one—said he had a mantra he repeated to himself: "It's the economy, stupid!" By this he meant that, all politics and publicity aside, it was the underlying performance of the national economy that determined his success as President. Couples ought to listen to similar advice: "It's the relationship, stupid!" In other words, what is really important is not your marital status or the ceremony you go through or what other people think or how you eat your wedding cake. The only thing that matters is how well you get along with your partner. This simple fact can easily get lost in a public ceremony.

When you find someone who you get along with, the relationship itself ought to be sufficient reward. Right? In most cases, though, there seems to be something amiss. If you fall in love with someone, move in with them and have sex with them on a regular basis, pretty soon things start becoming distressingly routine. "Is this all there is?" In your own fantasies and in the fairytales you have been fed since childhood, love was supposed to be a magical experience that enlivens your life forever. Reality, however, will probably give you something different, probably a life that is just as routine and boring as it was before you fell in love.

When something seems to be missing, people look around them to try to figure out what it is. If love right now isn't perfect bliss, what do we need to do to make it happen? What is the magic ingredient that is lacking?

"I know, we need to get married!"

You may not have a clear understanding as to how this is going to improve the relationship, but if your parents did it and your grandparents did it and all your friends are doing it, maybe you should, too. Maybe living in a relationship just for "now" isn't sufficient. Maybe the one missing link between you and eternal happiness is to stand up before family and friends and make a permanent public declaration.

If people know, deep within them, that this reasoning doesn't make sense, it might help explain why the ceremony itself has to get so complicated. If you are going to invest in magic, then you want to pile on as much magic as possible!

If you are not completely satisfied with your out-of-wedlock relationship, there are two directions you can go: You can pull away from it, or you can dive deeper into it, thinking that what you need is more commitment and less choice. Diving deeper is usually a lot easier than pulling back. At least it seems like an exciting adventure while pulling back can involve painful rejection, awkward disentanglement and a lot of hurt feelings—and then you are alone once again. If you are only vaguely dissatisfied, unclear on your own goals, afraid of loneliness and don't know what to do, which direction are you going to go? Deeper, probably!

The legal path between unmarried and married is really quite simple: You go to the courthouse and get a marriage license; you bring it to a justice of the peace or a certified clergy member who takes your vows; this official then signs a certificate of marriage, which is filed permanently at the courthouse. Under the law, the only thing that proves you are married is that piece of paper on file at the local courthouse or city clerk's office.

If you went to Vegas, you could get these steps done quickly and with a minimum of expense, but that's much too easy for most people. If a ceremony is expected to change things, then it has to be complicated. If this magical theatrical event is supposed to be a symbolic representation of the progression of the relationship, then it has to display obvious substance if the relationship is expected to improve.

There is a recurring philosophy often expressed in various ways by couples about to be married: "No pain, no gain." If you want a relationship to succeed, they say, then you have to be willing to make sacrifices.

Is "no pain, no gain" a valid philosophy? Well, yes and no. Sometimes, you do have to make sacrifices for things that are important to you. The mistake is thinking that pain and sacrifice alone will guarantee success. People who subscribe to the "no pain, no gain" philosophy will deliberately put themselves through complex or painful ordeals on the false assumption that it makes the end product more valuable.

Some gain requires pain, but pain doesn't guarantee gain. Making a wedding ceremony more complicated is a pain of sorts, but it doesn't do anything to improve success in the years that follow.

"It's the relationship, stupid!"

Charles' and Diana's Wedding Disaster

We now return to one of the enduring mysteries of matrimony: What caused the breakup of Prince Charles and Lady Diana? Was it Charles' affair with Camilla that put the nails in the coffin, or was it Diana's emotional instability? While Charles eventually admitted the affair, he said that he engaged in it only after the marriage had already broken down. Diana, however, claimed spousal abuse.

She told the press: "My husband made me feel inadequate in every possible way. Each time I came up for air he pushed me down again."

Rather than jumping into the debate of who did what to whom, I prefer to set aside the charges and countercharges and look at the marriage from a systems perspective. As I crunch the numbers and analyze the balance of power, I see that this couple was already doomed on their wedding day.

I was there! I witnessed the ceremony along with 750 million other viewers—perhaps the largest television audience in history. Even at my tender age, I knew that something was wrong. It seemed less a joyous celebration than a royal funeral.

There was the terrified bride, only a month out of her teens, arriving in a horse-drawn carriage in a £9000 gown, surrounded by all the pomp and symbolism money could buy. There was the groom, decked out in a military uniform with all the power of the crown behind him. The fate of the British Empire hung in the balance, as Charles was already 32 and had yet to produce an heir.

It was a "fairytale wedding" the announcers said, over and over. With the blessings of the Queen, the bride's family, the Houses of Parliament of both Britain and Canada and the prayers and good wishes of millions, you'd think that the marriage had everything going for it.

Apparently not. Something got lost in this ceremony. Something got run over.

"It's the relationship, stupid!"

With so much riding on this union, so many external expectations heaped upon it, how did either Charles or Diana have any chance to be themselves? Diana was a child. Charles was an older child. They didn't know what they wanted. They only knew what was expected of them.

This seemed to be love. He was a dashing prince. She was innocent, charming and showed little personal direction. The slipper seemed to fit.

What went wrong is the same thing going wrong in a thousand weddings taking place this very moment: the confusion of external symbolism with functional operation.

Being a prince has nothing to do with it. The size of the engagement ring has nothing to do with it. Even sex can become boring as hell after you've done it for the umpteenth time. In the end, all that matters is how well two genderless, powerless humans get along with each other when sharing close quarters.

Even siblings have trouble with that. If you live too close to anyone for too long, you want to throttle them. Working out the boundary issues is really complicated, and there's nothing the Queen or Houses of Parliament can do to help.

You have to have interests and philosophy in common. You

have to have a natural rapport that's entirely private and can't be represented in a public ceremony. Is this someone with whom you would get along as a disembodied brain sitting in the jar next to yours? If not, the relationship is bound to go bust.

If you want to see true love, look at Charles and Camilla. In 2005, they finally tied the knot. Did anyone notice? It took 30 years to get there, but maybe the delay was all for the best. Here's a relationship that happened by itself, for itself, without the sanction or approval of anyone.

When the Queen and Houses of Parliament finally gave their blessing, the couple was like "So what?"

This is our relationship, not yours.

Commitment and Negotiation

Commitment.

It is a word you hear a lot at weddings and from people who are about to wed. They say, "I am getting married to express my commitment to my partner." "Commitment," in this context, is supposed to mean dedication or loyalty.

The word has other meanings however. If you "commit" a crime you may be "committed" to prison. Once you are in prison, however, you wouldn't say that you were "committed" to your cellmate. It isn't loyalty or dedication that keeps you together. A more accurate description is that you are "imprisoned" together.

Commitment, in the sense of voluntary loyalty, is certainly an essential part of life. You can't accomplish anything substantial, in any domain, without pledging a certain amount of your future attention to it. The question is whether commitment can be nailed down forever in a public ceremony. It is like capturing a butterfly and pinning it in a case. In the process of trying to preserve it, you are also killing it. Can commitment—the voluntary kind—really be pinned down forever without turning it into imprisonment?

The betrothed may tell you, "I know marriage won't always be easy. There could be problems from time to time, but I am committed to resolving them. There is no reward without sacrifice."

Yes, there will be problems, because you will have merged

your finances and created a new corporate entity you are not used to. Yes, you will probably find a way to "resolve" any problems between you because you don't have much choice. They won't necessarily be healthy resolutions, though; perhaps you'll just be sweeping problems under the carpet to be dealt with later.

If you are trapped in a prison cell with someone full-time, you are tempted to solve problems with temporary, superficial fixes rather than any deep surgery. If your cellmate has sensitivities, you are going to learn to tiptoe around them, because you know the wrath you'll earn for saying or doing the wrong thing. When you are trapped in a cage with a tiger, you don't think much about the long-term health of the relationship; you only want to avoid being eaten right now.

Your motivation would seem purer if you had your own home and your friend had theirs and every day, through no formal obligation, you went over to see your friend. Then you could truthfully say that you were "committed" to them. If the two of you had a fight, you could withdraw to your respective homes and not see each other for a while. If you both found you missed each other and that there was still value in the relationship, you would probably be drawn back together, provided you could resolve the problem that pushed you apart.

People who get married assume that love and positive reinforcement can solve every problem. They can't. In every long-term relationship, problems will inevitably arise where the only effective solution is withdrawal.

Let's say your partner is drinking too much, to the point where you feel it is interfering in your relationship. Or maybe the problem is not something bad or destructive, just something your partner does or doesn't do that diminishes your interest in them. If you are free to withdraw, then you will. You try to make it clear to them what the issue is, then you pull back to your own independent life.

Maybe this will be a permanent withdrawal or only a temporary one. At the time you pull back, you don't need to know. All you know is that the behavior has to change for the relationship to be comfortable to you and that talk alone hasn't helped. Even if you think the withdrawal will be temporary, you need to have the permanent option in your arsenal. Then you are in a strong negotiating position.

I regret to inform you: Love can be war sometimes! No matter how much you may be attracted your partner in the beginning, the ultimate success of the relationship will probably be determined by how well you fight. It may be all milk and honey at first, but sooner or later, your partner is going to head in some direction you object to. Either you are going to renegotiate or the relationship has to end.

If you are trapped in a cell with someone, then you are in a very weak negotiating position. You can say, "If you don't stop drinking, I'm leaving you," but things have to get really bad before you are likely to follow through on the threat. If you've already merged your finances and loudly declared the permanence of your relationship to the world, then no withdrawal can be graceful.

Instead you make compromises. You start making excuses for your partner's behavior instead of setting boundaries on what you will accept. You wimp out and opt for appeasement over confrontation, because you don't have much choice.

Negotiation is what a long-term relationship is all about! Eventually, you will want certain things while your partner wants different things. You negotiate and hopefully come to some sort of workable compromise. To be able to negotiate, you have to retain some independent power. It may be hard to think of love as a power struggle, especially when you are new to it, but it is! Fact is, a total merging is neither possible nor desirable. No matter how close you may become to someone, negotiation requires that you have one foot firmly planted outside the relationship, in an independent life where you don't need them at all.

Having your own independent life is a source of power that can help you squeeze the concessions you want out of the one you love. You wouldn't expect any less of them! If they are strong, too, then you will find an honorable middle ground. Healthy love is a form of ongoing conflict, hopefully more of a chess game than open warfare. The important thing is to play by the rules.

Think about the court system. When people go to court, they are fighting over something. The court system works because there is a standardized system for resolving these conflicts. The court is a "conflict resolution system," and the healthy functioning of society depends on how well this system works. If your marriage falls apart, you might find yourself in the public court system, but every relationship should have its own conflict resolution system in private. When you have a conflict with your partner, what is the proper process you should go through to fix it? When you are fighting, all you are usually thinking about is the current bone of contention. What is more important, however, is the *manner* in which you fight.

The most powerful tool of negotiation is withdrawal. To be able to negotiate on substantial issues, you need to have the ability to pull back, away from the relationship, even if you don't actually do it. If the person you are negotiating with knows you are trapped, you probably won't get much change out of them. If they know you are free to move and perhaps take away something they want, then they are likely to be more responsive.

We like to think of relationships as involving only love, but relationships also involve power. No matter how tender you are with each other, there is a power struggle going on behind the scenes. You are constantly pushing and pulling at each other. Sometimes, you can verbalize what you want and solve a problem with words alone, and sometimes you can't. If you have weapons at your disposal, sometimes you have to actually use them, not just threaten to.

Divorce is a nuclear weapon. It is withdrawal without any hope of recovery. Unfortunately, it is difficult to negotiate with only nuclear weapons in your arsenal, since the only possible outcome is total annihilation. It is easier to negotiate with small arms—you know: bombs, guns, hand grenades, knives. In love, the weapons can be relatively gentle, as in, "Sorry, I don't want to do that, so I am not going with you."

If I have my independent life and you have yours, and I decide not to see you for a few days, it's no big deal. Maybe I am sending you a message about something I want to change, but I'm not saying that the relationship is over. It's just that we come together when we have things in common and pull apart when we don't. If we are important to each other and truly "committed" to each other, then we will always be drawn back—no public declaration needed.

Things are different if the two of us have merged our practical lives to the point where casual withdrawal is impossible. If you are married, and your spouse takes off for a few days, it *is* a big deal. You'll want to know where they've gone and what they've done. Feelings may be hurt and jealousies may arise. Any withdrawal in this case seems like a loss of the commitment you loudly announced in the beginning.

Remember those vows you made on your wedding day—joined "'Til death do you part." That may not have been the exact wording, but no one stands up before all their family and friends and says, "I pledge to stay with this person whenever it is convenient and for only as long as the relationship is really working." That's probably the healthier position, but it's not the way the magic talisman of marriage is supposed to work. Marriage means you are living permanently with someone "for better or worse," even when you aren't getting along with them. Anything else is going to be seen by the world as a failure of the marriage.

If you hadn't made this loud declaration in front of family and friends, then occasional withdrawal wouldn't seem like a big thing. It would just be part of the natural ebb and flow of the relationship.

Let's not pretend to believe in fairytales. Love is war. It is negotiation. If what you want is important and you don't get it, then you take your ball and go home.

Love and Enabling

There is a fine line between love and enabling.

"Love," in most of its forms, is a decision to set aside your own needs, at least temporarily, and focus on someone else's. This can be romantic love, maternal love, love for your country or love for any creature weaker than you who seems to need your protection. Love in itself is noble and inevitable. At some point in our lives, we have to look outside ourselves for meaning and satisfaction.

But love is risky. Whenever you lower your defenses and try to serve someone else, there's a chance you will be abused or imprisoned. It is also possible your well intentioned actions may be counter productive and end up hurting the one you wanted to help.

"Enabling" is reinforcing someone's dysfunctional behavior by providing an environment in which it can continue. We may speak of an alcoholic being enabled by their well-meaning spouse who cleans up their messes and protects them from the hardest consequences of their actions. The alcoholic does the drinking, but the spouse provides the safe environment in which it can take place.

Love and enabling form a Yin and Yang. Whenever you engage in the former, you must grapple with the potential for the latter.

The simplest example of love is a parent's care for their child. No one would question the need to protect a toddler from the dangers of the world; yet, in doing so the parent is creating an artificial expectation that is a source of danger in itself. One of the universal traumas of human existence is escaping from the bubble of protected childhood into a "real" world that is vastly different.

Every gift you give has a cost. Any charity given without strings can quickly become an entitlement, where the recipient feels he deserves the support without having to win it himself. This only heightens the trauma when the gift is eventually withdrawn and the subject has to deal with reality in its unbuffered form.

We all know it would be cruel to raise a dog or cat in a comfortable home then dump it in the wild to fend for itself, yet people who have extra resources routinely set their children up for a similar trauma. If you raise a kid in an environment of relative wealth and privilege—filled with Santa Clauses and Easter Bunnies and magical parents who provide everything— how will he ever adapt to a world without magic?

Romantic relationships are no less risky. When you fall in love, you inevitably want to share resources, and this sharing becomes routine and expected after a while. An ideal romantic relationship is one of equality, where both parties have something valuable to give and the exchange of services is nearly equal, but this is a difficult condition to maintain. Things may seem stable when resources are plentiful and neither party has any reason to change. The system breaks down, however, when one party's dysfunction clashes with the demands of the outside world.

When a person faces a choice between changing their own behavior or drawing on the common pot, the pot seems so much easier. This is particularly a problem in the case of addiction. The addiction is reinforced by anxiety and fear, and only anxiety and fear can counter it. When you offer someone artificial protection from the consequences of their own behavior, their anxiety is reduced and so is their motivation to change.

We all have our addictions—if not a chemical substance then some delusional misperception of the world based on our own emotional needs. The main thing that keeps this dysfunction in check is unprotected interaction with the outside world, which gives us hard, undeniable feedback whenever we misjudge it. When a relationship provides a buffer between us and outside reality, regulation becomes much more difficult. If we don't have the freedom to withdraw, we must resort to trying to change our loved one's behavior using words alone, which are weak weapons against addiction.

Love is not just love but war. At some point, the person you love is also going to be your opponent. Protection is going to morph into enabling, and you're going to have to find a way to withdraw that support—for the other person's good as well as your own.

Yes, a toddler needs protection, but only up to a point. If the ultimate goal is full exposure to reality, you have to let as much reality in as possible. A lesson with words is nowhere near as effective as a sunburn or a pinched finger justly earned. As the child gets older, you protect him from less and less of reality until, hopefully, he can stand on his own.

The adult you fall in love with should *already* stand on his own, and it is a mistake to let him fall back on you as a crutch. Whenever you fall in love, you need to know your boundaries and retain control over your own resources. Love may be unconditional, but what you give of yourself shouldn't be.

Sooner or later, each person must suffer the consequences of his own actions. There is no way around it. If you stand in the way for too long, all your energy will be sucked into the black hole of their need, without any change to show for it.

Love Can't Change Personality

Love can seem magical in the short term, but in the long term it can't change someone's core personality.

"Personality" is an individual's habitual style of dealing with the world. This is expressed in their interests, their political opinions, the way they communicate, what they communicate about, how they spend their free time and how they respond to the problems of life. Personality is a person's recurring patterns of behavior and perception, expressed across a wide variety of circumstances. It can also be thought of as a person's unique mental illness, dictating their delusions and the kind of self-destructive mistakes they are likely to make.

Let's say you are waiting at an airport gate for an outgoing flight that has been delayed (as I am doing as I write this). As the delay stretches from minutes into hours, you begin to see what your fellow travelers are made of. Some people repeatedly go to the gate podium to complain. The longer the delay is, the angrier they become. Other people pull out books or laptop computers and start using them. They figure that if they are going to be delayed, they might as well use the time wisely. Still other people head for the airport bar and wait for the flight there, and here in Las Vegas some spend the time in front of slot machines conveniently located near the gate.

How someone responds to a stressor like this is an expression of their personality. The operating style of the angry people is fundamentally different from those who take advantage of the time. Under a similar level of stress in entirely different circumstances, you can expect that each of these people will respond in a similar way.

If you have raised children, you know that each of them has their own style, which starts becoming apparent at an early age. There are colicky babies and calm ones. There are children who like dolls, those who like to take things apart, those who prefer sports, those who whine a lot, those who are quiet and self-contained and those who talk non-stop. The older a child gets, the more pronounced and stable their traits become.

By the end of high school, teachers have a pretty good idea where each kid is headed. One kid will probably be doing mechanical work for most of his life, like auto repair. Another kid is destined to be an artist. A third is a charismatic leader and a born manager. Another, if he hasn't dropped out of school already, will probably be a scam artist or lifelong drug addict. The exact career path each kid follows remains to be seen, but by the time of graduation, you have a pretty good idea of his lifelong predilections.

We can argue about how much of one's personality comes from nature (genes) and how much from nurture (environment and upbringing). If you discover, at the age of 35, that you have an identical twin sibling you didn't know about, and you visit them, you will probably find both uncanny similarities and striking differences between you. This would be a graphic illustration of the nature vs. nurture issue. Your similarities are probably an expression of your genes, while your differences are an expression of the different environments you grew up in and the different opportunities you had.

Personality is a quality of behavior, not of appearance, but the body you were born into is inevitably going to shape your personality because it affects how people respond to you and what you are physically good at. A boy with a linebacker's physique is likely to become a linebacker and not try out for ballet. Someone with a ballerina's physique isn't going to become a Sumo wrestler, and the boy who looks like a Sumo is going to be treated like one, no matter how gentle his demeanor. It is often a cruel hand biology deals, but the characteristics of our body can't help but influence how people treat us and our methods of interacting with the world.

Personality also embodies one's unique perception of reality. You may think there is only one reality, but in fact reality differs greatly from person to person. One person, raised in a relatively warm and benevolent environment, might perceive the world as basically fair and just, while another, the product of a less stable childhood, might regard the world as inherently treacherous and deceptive. The real world, in fact, is more complex than either prediction. Each is a personality judgment.

Fundamental self-worth is contained in one's personality. Is a person highly self-confident, or do they feel themselves worthless and expect to be cheated? Do they fundamentally distrust all parental figures or all members of the opposite sex? Do they have an impulsive need to defy authority? Do they have a fundamental belief in the goodness of others? These are all instinctual operating theories that will have a profound effect on a person's relations with the world.

Personality defies language. You cannot dissuade someone of their fundamental beliefs using words alone. We are used to communicating with each other in words, and if we all speak the same language, we tend to assume that we all understand each other. This is true only for physical objects. If you say, "Put the red ball in the blue box" when both the ball and the box are present, everybody knows what you mean. Language becomes far less effective when you try to talk about less tangible things like relationships.

What, for example, does "love" mean? It is going to mean different things to different people based on their background and personality. In fact, nearly all the language commonly used to discuss relationships is open to interpretation. The language of relationships might have sentimental value when used in a greeting card or a popular song, but it is pretty much useless for getting anything done.

If I say, "You are selfish and immature and don't understand me at all!" the only thing I have really conveyed to you is my own emotional unhappiness. I haven't provided any useful information about how to be less selfish and immature or how to understand me better. That's where language breaks down. "Be more mature," isn't an adequate instruction from me to you, because you probably believe you are already mature and have been doing things the best you can.

At the beginning of a romantic relationship, couples think they are in sync with each other when they exchange relationship words like "I love you." In fact, each may be interpreting the words in entirely different ways. Only later, in times of stress, do you realize how much the interpretations have diverged and how useless language is for changing anything.

You can give your partner specific physical instructions on one thing you want changed—like "Pick up your own clothes!"—and they may indeed try to change, but they will probably miss all the other circumstances that concern you, like their attitude toward cleanliness. What you may find over time is that you are both speaking the same verbal language— English—but that no real communication is taking place.

Unfortunately, there is no real cure for these communication breakdowns, because each of your personalities is already stable. One of the basic laws of relationships is: Nothing you can say or do will change another adult's personality. It is a hard lesson to accept, especially if you are romantically bonded to someone and have invested a lot of your resources in them. You can try to change a specific behavior, but you are never going to turn a messy person into a neat one or an irresponsible cad into a devoted partner. If you have already made an investment, you may try changing them anyway, but you are probably going to fail in the end.

Who should you look for in a long-term partner? Here is a little relationship advice: Choose someone whose personality is as close as possible to yours! If you can find your missing identical twin, they would be ideal! You don't have to have the same background, career or outward appearance, but you do need to have the same basic worldview. Then there will be fewer gaps in your communication. Don't believe the nonsense that "Opposites attract." Opposites may attract, but they also tend to annihilate each other!

Unfortunately, it can be hard to tell if the person is like you or unlike you when you are emotionally involved with them. Lovers *always* find things magically in common with each other, thanks to selective attention. You may have to interact with someone for a while before you identify the most important similarities and differences.

Even if you meet someone whose personality seems to match yours, it is only a matter of time before your perspectives start to diverge. After spending years with someone, you are bound to see aspects of their personality you weren't aware of when you first met them. When this happens, you will face some hard choices: Do you try to change the personality, accommodate it or get out of the relationship altogether?

The more invested someone already is in the relationship, the more they attempt the first and second options: trying to change their partner or accommodating them. Neither is likely to yield promising results. Change rarely happens, and accommodation tends to be a creeping disease that gets worse with time: The more you accommodate, the more accommodation is expected.

The most you can hope for is to change a specific behavior. We know this is possible because law enforcement manages to do it. The threat of a prison sentence is reasonably effective in keeping people from committing crimes, even if their personality predisposes them to. Outward behavior is changed when it is enforced by hard consequences, without the need for underlying personality changes.

If you can change your partner's behavior in the things that most distress you, that may be enough to preserve the relationship—if indeed the relationship is valuable enough to preserve. The catch is, it is hard to impose hard consequences from within a marriage. Compared to an outsider, you have few weapons and bargaining chips. You can talk; you can yell and you can threaten to leave, but these are weak weapons compared with actually walking out the door.

If you are free to walk, and you partner knows you are fully capable of making it stick, then you actually might get some change, not in personality but perhaps in a key disruptive behavior. If you don't get any change, then you have to say, "Sayonara!" and really go.

A seeming paradox of personality is that, although you can't change it from the outside, people can change it from within, by their own deliberate decision. The catch is, their pain usually has to be real and substantial before they figure things out. If you walk out the door and don't come back, your ex-partner may very well change their fundamental philosophy over time, but most likely only after you are long gone and have no intention of returning.

People change their own behavior and personality only by experiencing the direct consequences of their actions, and these consequences have to be "hard" to be effective. You can threaten to leave all you want, but significant change will only happen when you *actually* leave and there is a realistic chance you won't be back.

No matter how much you love someone, you should never give up your option of leaving them. It may be the most valuable tool you have.

The Power of Money

At the beginning of your relationship, during the peculiar hormonal process of falling in love, money seemed irrelevant. You were so thrilled to finally find your apparent soulmate that you were eager to share with them everything you had, often to an absurd degree. You often see it in sidewalk cafes: amorous couples feeding each other from their own plates like they were children. It doesn't matter whether I order the Combo Plate #1 and you get Combo #6 or the other way around, because we are both going to share each other's meal, generously and without conflict.

This sentiment lasts only during the courtship, after which natural territoriality begins to reassert itself. "Listen here: I ordered #1 because that's what I want, and I'll stab you with this fork if you try to take any of it! If you wanted #1, you should have ordered it yourself."

As a couple gets closer to each other, sharing eventually reaches a tipping point where it becomes awkward, uncomfortable and counterproductive. One way or another, we eventually realize there has to be a mechanism to hold each person responsible for their choices and actions. Without it, disequilibriums will emerge where one partner starts draining the resources of the other.

In reasonably successful marriages, pseudo-ownership rules are created, even if they have no legal standing. Certain objects or domains are labeled as "his" or "hers." She might "own" the bedroom while the garage is his territory. There is an understanding between them that each person has discretion over their domain and will not interfere in the other's without permission. This system works up to a point, as long as there are plenty of resources to go around. The system tends to fail when the going gets tough and difficult decisions have to be made in an area that isn't clearly his or hers—like the overall finances.

Informal boundaries also don't work when one or both partners have a problem with impulse control. And frankly *all* of us have problems with impulse control, just in different domains. Even the most disciplined athlete or scientist is bound to be undisciplined in other areas of his life. In these areas, he is still a child, and he needs to feel the hard consequences of his actions for his behavior to be controlled.

If an unmarried person has a weakness for gambling or shopping, they are going to keep doing it until they run out of money and their credit cards are maxed out. At that point, economic reality will curb their behavior. They simply can't shop or gamble anymore if they don't have any money or credit for it. The situation may be painful, but precisely because it is painful they will eventually learn to control their impulses.

When this person gets married, they now have a bigger pot of money and credit to draw from and a longer way to fall before they hit rock bottom. They don't have to face "hard" reality until they have burned through their partner's resources as well as their own. The partner has few mechanisms to counter this. They can offer only a "soft" reality that isn't nearly as powerful: verbal warnings, requests, ultimatums and pleadings.

You can try to draw a line in the sand and say, "I'm not giving any more than this"—but where should you draw this line and how do you enforce it? If I have my own paycheck which I deposit into an account that is only in my name, I can tell my spouse, "You can't have that money." Legally, however, this division is fictitious. Under marriage law, it is their money, too! If my spouse goes into my wallet without permission and takes a huge amount of money, it is not legally theft and cannot be prosecuted as such, because everything we have is community property.

Even if you retain control of your own checking account, your assets can be eroded in other ways. If your impulsive partner gambles away their own paycheck, that's his problem, but what if he fails to pay the electric bill as agreed? Is the non-gambling partner going to allow the power to be shut off? Probably not; they will grudgingly pay the bill from their own paycheck. Thereby, the impulsive partner receives no natural negative consequences for their action—going without electricity. When financial boundaries have been legally abolished, nearly all rules regarding money become likewise fuzzy, flexible and difficult to enforce.

If you never legally marry, your financial lives remain separate by default and you retain more discretion and control. Your partner gets your money only if you explicitly hand it to them. If you decide to share a residence, then you have to agree on how the rent and utilities will be paid, but beyond this, your money remains yours and theirs remains theirs.

If your partner blows their money on something frivolous and finds themselves broke, you can realistically say, "Oh, well!" and not give them a penny. On the other hand, you can choose to deliberately subsidize them if you find their situation meritorious. If you earn more than they do, it is reasonable for you to pay more of the common bills. You have to figure out your own formula, but you can do it thoughtfully and deliberately, according to the ongoing negotiations between you.

Retaining your own financial independence is a way to preserve natural and healthy personal boundaries. It doesn't necessarily mean you distrust your partner and expect them to take advantage of you. Things just work more smoothly when you control the product of your own labor. If nothing else, there is less bureaucracy to deal with, because you shouldn't need permission to spend your own money.

Merging your finances may seem harmless in the beginning. You say, "It's only money, and love is more important," but unless you have a huge excess of it, money is something you should not dismiss lightly. Money is power, responsibility and boundaries. It is a quantifier of your own labor and, to a certain extent, a measure of your worldly talent and discipline. If your money derives from your own labor, you should never surrender control of it, even to the one you love. Being responsible for your own money is like being responsible for your own health and career—a natural personal domain no one can or should take away from you.

For most of us without independent wealth, money is a regulating system that dictates much of what we do in our daily lives. Money, or lack thereof, forces most of us to work, and we will only participate in leisure activities we can financially afford. Money may be tyrannical and unfair, but at least it gives some default structure to our lives.

If money were to suddenly become meaningless, most people wouldn't know what to do with themselves. If all the beer was free, more people would drink too much of it. If everyone had all the money they needed, few would accomplish anything with their lives. People who have all the money they could want are often hedonistic and directionless and not all that happy. You may fantasize about all the noble things you might do if you didn't have to work, but in practice most people would squander their time on trivialities. Without money and its enforced inequities, little in society would get done.

A romantic partnership assumes there are better ways than

money to regulate people. This may indeed be true, but these methods have to be implemented and tested through actual experience. Theory alone isn't enough. You can't just abolish all monetary boundaries—like Communism tried to do—and expect people to know how to live with each other.

Romance tempts us with a new Communist Manifesto, expressed by Lennon not Lenin: "All you need is love." This may sound appealing in theory, but the ideal breaks down under any kind of real-world pressure. Love is not a regulating mechanism the way money is. Money eventually runs out and creates a solid incentive for action, but love is supposed to be boundless and never run out. What this means in real life—if you believe in Lennon—is you never know how much of your own resources you should give to the one you love.

When you erase the financial boundaries between two people, you are courting a sort of anarchy where neither party knows what their responsibilities are. Inevitably, some people give too little to the relationship and some people give too much. A Communist relationship may work satisfactorily when the community is rich and there are plenty of resources to smooth over inequities. Anarchy creeps in when the community starts running low on resources. That is when it becomes difficult to decide who is responsible for what and how much each party should sacrifice for the common good.

This is where the "security" and "protection" of marriage take on a darker meaning. When times get tough and the decisions become painful, it is easy for one partner to fall back on the relative strength and apparent security of the other. As long as the stronger partner is willing to give more, then the weaker partner is willing to take more, and this pattern tends to amplify with time. Once this protective-dependent cycle begins, there may be no easy way to stop it short of violent divorce.

Many marriages have disintegrated when one partner loses

their job and starts sitting around the house all day. They try to find work, but they don't try hard enough. They aren't forced to make any painful compromises because they have their partner to support them. The supporting partner is frustrated but has little power to force the other to change. Their threats are usually empty and their partner knows it. Nothing they say has the same power as natural reality—where someone gets evicted for not paying rent and has to sleep in the street if they don't produce anything.

That is the problem with any kind of safety net: If you offer it to people, they will probably use it, but not for the life-or-death situations you envisioned. Benevolent protection is often abused as an easy way to avoid personal responsibility, and over time it becomes an addiction. If one partner gets themselves in a difficult bind and the other dutifully rescues them, what happens next? The partner gets themselves into more messes, knowing rescue is sure to come.

The cycle often progresses to the point where the whole community ship is sinking, and the protective partner can't get the dependent one to take the impending crisis seriously. "We can't continue to spend more money than we're making!" they try to say. Addicted to protection, however, the dependent partner doesn't understand and expects the provider to take care of everything. The ship can't be sinking, they think, because the band is still playing.

We can't be broke because we still have credit cards!

The Credit Card of Life

Your first shiny new credit card is an exciting thing. You no longer have to carry cash but can just swipe the card. There is no finance charge if you pay the bill in full every month. If you don't, you only have to make a small minimum payment, with interest charged on the balance. The interest is usually 1-3% of the outstanding balance per month, which seems like a tiny amount at first. It is a wonderful feeling walking into a store with $10 in your pocket but a credit card that will let you spend $1000. What could possibly go wrong?

Even if we don't have a plastic credit card, each of us has received a sort of credit card at birth. You could call it your "future discretion account"—or as credit card companies would market it, your "Freedom Card." Actually, your Freedom Card is more like a debit card, with all the years of your life stored on it. Upon reaching adulthood, you can either pay as you go, deciding what to do with your life as it unfolds, or you can spend your future freedom all at once, maxing out your Freedom Card and using the rest of your life to pay it off.

Consumer credit is a way to spend your future freedom right now. Instead of waiting to enjoy the fruits of your labor, you can have them now based on the promise of your future labor. Credit lets you possess today the same car or house you would otherwise have to save for years for. The cost, however, can be incredibly high and may not be obvious at first. It is not just the accumulated interest, which could end up being far more than the original loan, but the fact that you are locking yourself into a personal future consistent with the payment plan you contracted to.

Even with zero-percent financing on your new car, the loan still demands you maintain an adequate salary to afford the payments, such as the job you were doing when you first applied. This commitment usually makes you less inclined to make big changes in your life. You stop taking chances and settle instead for a safe and comfortable routine that assures the commitments will be met.

Marriage is a bit like that. You are committing yourself to a lifelong payment plan, supposedly for the benefits you are receiving right away. No matter where your future life may take you, you are agreeing to take your partner with you. Whatever their strengths or weaknesses may be—their future assets and liabilities—you are agreeing to share them. On your wedding day, you have an idealistic plan for how this is all going to work. You think you know what is going to happen for the rest of your life, so why not commit to that plan now?

If you live in a society that accepts divorce, it all seems reversible. If the marriage doesn't become everything you hoped, you can always step out of it, right? Not so fast! Marriage is usually only the start of the spending spree. Each time you use your Freedom Card, using it becomes easier, until you are charging away big hunks of your future freedom without batting an eyelash.

A couple needs a place to live, so once they are married it seems only natural they should own their own home. Out comes the Freedom Card and—Swipe!—they now have a 20-year mortgage. The new house needs to be filled with furniture, so—Swipe! Swipe!—it magically appears. Even filled with furniture, though, the place feels lonely. Your Freedom Card can solve that too: Swipe! Swipe! Swipe! Soon you hear the patter of little feet! It seems there's nothing your Freedom

Card can't help you with.

From time to time we read in the news about a crime spree: Someone robs a convenience store and gets away with it so he continues committing crimes in an ever-escalating pattern. Soon he is stealing cars and robbing banks, maybe even taunting the police to catch him. Overcoming his inhibitions in one crime just makes it easier to commit bigger ones.

In fact, previous crimes almost demand new crimes. Robbing the first convenience store is an investment of sorts, an emotional commitment the criminal cannot back out of. The easiest way to justify one's past mistakes is repeat them more flamboyantly. Expanding the questionable activity is a way of quashing the anxiety of doubt. While the criminal may have gotten away with the first crime, the authorities almost always catch up with him later because he can't stop doing it and leaves himself no way out.

Perhaps the greatest danger in using your Freedom Card for something seemingly reversible like marriage is that it reduces your inhibitions to future use. There has hardly ever been a wedding that hasn't been followed by a "commitment spree" of other obligations that freeze the marriage in place. Real estate, possessions, pets, children. Every new commitment you enter into with your spouse seems to justify the previous ones. And because it makes the relationship harder to back out of, it certainly reinforces the marriage vows—for better or worse!

These are the liabilities that divorce courts have to disentangle. Marriage itself can be dissolved with the wave of a judge's hand, but the shared financial commitments built upon it are not so easily undone. Because the couple is now a corporation it is impossible to tell whose debt is whose, so in the absence of an agreement, assets and liabilities are divided down the middle. This gets complicated with things like houses, cars or children which cannot be individually divided.

Divorce is far more complicated than marriage because you have to make an inventory of all these burdens and haggle over how they will be split, usually with the help of some very expensive lawyers.

Thanks to your Freedom Card, burning a hole in your naïve young pocket, it is easy to commit yourself to a set of future activities far beyond what you can reasonably predict. This happens to young people regardless of marriage. They say, "I don't see any reason I would want to change" and commit themselves to a payment plan consistent with that observation. Marriage only makes it easier to get in over one's head because responsibility is now distributed. You may be able to enforce discipline on yourself but imposing it on your partner is next to impossible.

We all know how money cries out to be spent when we have a little extra of it. When we have some in our pocket, prudence says we should sock it away, but we rarely do, because the world is filled with too many temptations. This impulse is relatively harmless when you are living from paycheck to paycheck, but it is incredibly dangerous when a credit card lets you spend future paychecks. Credit in all its forms makes you think you have more money than you do, so you tend to spend far more. It's great for the economy, perhaps, but not so great for you in the long run.

What you are spending, in fact, is future discretion—the freedom to adapt to changes in the world and yourself that you cannot now predict. Committed to a marriage, mortgage and all the accoutrements, you have created a straightjacket for yourself and there are a lot of directions you can no longer move. For example, if the local economy falters, you may not be able to sell the house. You did not anticipate this turn of events at the time you signed the mortgage, but that doesn't mean it won't happen.

History is full of unpredictable change. It has always

happened and always will. If you have maxed out your Freedom Card, you could have great difficulty responding to the next unexpected crisis. You can no longer move agilely like you could when you were paying cash—spending only what you had and deciding your life on a monthly basis.

A couple who is not married and who pay cash for everything may seem a little dull from the outside. All they have is who they are right now. No promises, no public announcements, no big commitments, just current reality. Dull, however, is a lot better than false prosperity that cannot last.

Children

There are two kinds of children: those who exist and those who don't. I am supportive of the former and opposed to the latter. In my opinion, children who do not exist should stay that way.

In fact, my proposal to the Interstellar Galactic Federation is that they put a total freeze on all human conceptions until this planet works out its problems. I am sure there are aliens somewhere in the universe who have this technology. A little block on the testes of 3 billion males should do the trick. Why should humans be allowed to bring new children into the world when there are so many already here who are not being adequately cared for?

If you have been considering making a baby, please, *please* think things through. It is an even more fateful and potentially debilitating decision than marriage. The world has its massive problems, but instead of addressing them, you would be creating a whole *new* problem—another mouth to feed and brain to educate and a new set of risks that didn't previously exist. In my opinion, voluntary childbirth is an exercise in vanity. You hope to create a little Mini Me who will worship you and follow in your footsteps. Trouble is, this little project almost never turns out as you hope. Sooner or later, he gets his own ideas and screws up your plans.

Now that childbirth is optional, not inevitable, when two people fall in love, why do they have babies at all? I think they do it for the same reason they get married: because there is a vague dissatisfaction in their life they are trying to fill up. You fell in love and moved in with your partner, but you still felt empty, so what was missing? Must be marriage! When you get married and your life stills lacks meaning and direction, what could be lacking? Must be children!

Oh, you'll have direction then! Guaranteed! Twenty-plus years of direction!

Will you have meaning? That's a different question. You'll certainly be occupied, but being busy does not necessarily prove your life is meaningful or that you have improved the world with your busyness. It is more like filling in a hole that you yourself dug.

It is so much purer, morally, to contribute to the upbringing of a child who is already here. He can be your own biological child! I am okay with that as long as the choice to bring him into the world has already passed. As I say, I got no problem with children who already exist and who need to be cared for. You can't put them back in the womb.

However, children who are already here can greatly complicate the problems of romance. Ideally, you should conduct your romantic relationship by itself, for itself, without external entanglements. If the two of you are substantially beneficial to each other, you stay together. Whenever things don't work, you draw apart. This is far more difficult if you've got a nest of little hatchlings to feed and it takes the resources of both of you to get it done. The parental relationship is unconditional, and you can't walk out on them.

Children can place you in the potential dilemma where you know your romantic relationship isn't working but you stay together anyway "for the children." Now you're in a fine kettle o' fish! I wish I had an easy solution for you, but I don't. Whatever way you go, it's ugly.

I can tell you how most people solve the dilemma. If the romantic relationship isn't working but their whole world is resting on it, they convince themselves that it *is* working and do their best to make it appear so. They don't perceive that they have a choice, so they just soldier on. The physiological bond between the two of you is probably still there, even if no real communication is taking place, so why not pretend this is all you ever wanted?

Pretending may seem to be enough. If you pile on enough roses, chocolates and sentimental words, it almost seems like you still have a real relationship. What you may no longer have, however, is your independent and reliable advisor— your second brain. Over time, your advisor may learn the same lesson you have learned to keep the peace: Tell your partner exactly what they want to hear.

People in an emotional bind like this can use a lot of smoke and mirrors to make their relationship seem viable. I have done it myself, and I'm not saying it is wrong! If you entered into a contract to raise children, then you must fulfill it by whatever means are available. Divorce may be impractical. More likely, though, it is simply unthinkable. Responsible people may not perceive it as an option, since it seems to go against those vows they made on their wedding day *and* the vows they made to their children. Unless they are forced into divorce by circumstances beyond their control, the logistical and emotional Armageddon of it seems too much to deal with. Instead, the problem is "solved" by never-ending appeasement, accommodation and submersion of one's own interests.

It is a mistake, however, to think you have no choice. The unthinkable must be fairly considered. If the romantic relationship isn't working—to the same standard you would expect if you had no children—then you shouldn't fool yourself into thinking it is. If the regime is oppressive, you should be looking for opportunities to escape. You should never let yourself be broken or try to suppress what you know is true. If the romantic relationship isn't working, then your children *will* know it—at least on some unconscious emotional level. In some way, it is messing up their psychology, and the damage may linger for generations.

Divorce can be incredibly painful, but so is open heart surgery. Sometimes, band-aids and analgesics don't work. Sometimes you have to dive in with scalpel and fix the problem at its source. Surgery is painful for everyone in the short term, but it may be better than a dull and unsolvable dysfunction that goes on for years.

I am not saying I have an easy solution or that I am recommending divorce. I have been there, so I know how hard it can be. All I'm saying is you can't just sweep things under the carpet. You cannot stay together "for the children" and not expect the children to be damaged by it.

Can you raise children without marriage? At least in Western countries you can. Plenty of unmarried couples are doing it now. It is a fallacy to think you need marriage to create a proper environment for child rearing. You do need a strong and stable relationship because it is destined for many trials, but stability does not imply legal marriage. On the contrary, it matters more that the parents have worked out their own boundary issues, including the financial ones. You don't build good boundaries by erasing boundaries, as marriage does.

Does the law care whether Mommy and Daddy are married? Not at all! In modern law in most Western countries, the rights and obligations of parenthood have been completely separated from marriage. Marriage gains you no additional rights and does not change child support obligations. It is the child's birth certificate, not the marriage certificate, that shows who is responsible.

Do the children care whether Mommy and Daddy are

married? For that matter, do they care if they have two Daddies or two Mommies? Of course not, especially if this is all the children have ever known. What does filter down to them is whether their parents truly love each other or are merely tolerating each other. The quality of the relationship between parents is communicated in so many ways that it is virtually impossible to hide.

If the parents are out of sync, they shouldn't be working together! Two parents are worse than one if the two are undermining each other's decisions. That is why courts usually assign primary custody to one parent or the other when the two are at war. If sharing didn't work when they were living together, it probably won't work when they are living apart.

So many dilemmas! So many minefields! It is a wonder any of us survived our own childhood!

Advisors and Sycophants

Couples like to think of marriage as uniting their strengths. He has certain special talents, and she has hers, so together they must have twice the abilities, right? Unfortunately, they aren't seeing the other half of the equation: Marriage can unite and reinforce the weaknesses of two people. If they each have different vulnerabilities, they could end up twice as vulnerable.

Each person has their own delusions—self-serving beliefs about life that are supported more by emotion than fact. For example, almost any hobby can be seen as delusional. If you like to go fishing, someone who isn't afflicted with this disease can innocently ask, "Why? What are you accomplishing by it apart from killing time and torturing fish?" If you are already invested in fishing, then you are not going to listen to these naysayers. You will go fishing as long and as often as you have resources to do so.

In real life, a happy marriage involves an implicit understanding that you are not going to challenge each other's delusions. Even if you disagree with something your partner does, as long as it doesn't intrude into your own space you are likely to keep quiet about it. Because you know it is unproductive to fight it, you let them fish!

A tee-shirt in a fishing shop reads: "My wife told me if I go fishing one more time she's going to leave me. I'm sure going to miss her!" This is truer than you might suppose. If you criticized your partner every time they indulged their delusions, the marriage wouldn't last long. The more you are trapped together, the more you are likely to accommodate rather than challenge. Honest and independent intellectual exchange is compromised by the need to keep the peace.

After a hard day at the office, a husband comes home to his wife and recounts all the problems of the day. Whatever he says, he expects his wife to agree with him. He naturally desires only soothing words not more opposition. He doesn't expect her to repeat the same criticisms he already received at the office.

The wife, in turn, wants to believe in her husband because she has already invested so much in him. If there is a conflict between her husband and forces in the outside world, the outside forces must be at fault. The only data the wife has received about the conflicts at work comes from her husband. This is like a lawyer coming into court and recounting his side of a conflict without the opposing side having any opportunity to speak. Given what her husband has told her, naturally she is going to agree with him. "Of course you are right, dear," she says.

There would be hell to pay if the wife disagreed with her husband. The conflicts of the office would be carried into the bedroom, and there would be no rest for either party. Instead, the wife is more likely to agree wholeheartedly and might even come up with a few new reasons why he must be right. The next day, the husband goes back to work, reinforced in the righteousness of his position... and makes a jerk of himself!

A sycophant is someone who tells the boss whatever he wants to hear. "Of course you are right," they tell him in every instance. This may sound nice and feel comforting, but it isn't preparing the boss for the eventual intrusion of reality. Ideally, what you want in a relationship is a truly independent advisor, not a sycophant.

To best prepare for reality, you need an advisor who will tell you when you are wrong but who can also fairly recognize when you are doing things right. This kind of unbiased advice is much more difficult to recruit and maintain than a sycophant or even an enemy. The advisor must care about you and know you well enough to speak your language but not be so invested in you that they can't see your weaknesses. It is a difficult balance to maintain.

Your advisor will lose their independence if you are trapped together in a cell with no hope of escape. To be truly effective as a critic, an advisor needs to be able drop an unpleasant truth then pull back and let it sink in. If the criticism is truly valid, then the person being criticized is likely to be angry or confused. They need time to sort things out without the advisor lurking over them.

Personal growth takes time. If you have an argument with your partner, and you score some good points, the best thing you can do is withdraw and let those points be absorbed. If you remain under foot, then the immediate quality of interaction is probably going to degenerate and your good points could be forgotten.

If you go away, then your partner has a chance to think things through on their own. The pacing now should be up to them. If the criticism is valid, they need time to processes it and come up with a new plan. It the criticism is invalid, they need time to assemble a defense. They will come back to you when they have generated a new synthesis and are ready for your feedback again.

If you have been working on a project for a long time, you are going to be emotionally invested in it. A dutiful, sycophantic spouse is going to say, "It's wonderful, dear!" regardless of whether it really is, but that's not the kind of feedback you need. You need someone who will give you an accurate picture of reality without being tainted by too much investment.

Truly useful and independent criticism is something you have to carefully cultivate. Your partner needs to trust you enough to say what they really think without fear of you biting their head off. If you respond badly to criticism even once, it could shut down the feedback machine and rob you of useful data in the future. If you reinforce and reward useful criticism, it is more likely to happen again.

When the two of you are in conflict, whatever you are fighting about will soon be forgotten. What is important in the long term is *how* you fight—i.e. your rules of engagement. This in itself should be a matter of debate between you, and it should be practiced on minor issues before the major ones come along. If I want Italian food and you want Chinese, by what methodology should we resolve this conflict?

In the long run, this is what makes or breaks relationships: not what we have in common but how we manage our differences. When you disagree, will you do it honorably, or will you do it in such a way that it suppresses future criticism.

When a messenger bears bad news, will you shoot him or let him in? That depends a lot on whether the messenger is free to leave. In practice, the messengers most likely to get shot are actually the ones we are closest to, because we know they can't leave us even with a few bullets in them.

The Evolution of Needs

When we are poor, all we can think about is money. We become preoccupied with it, and when an opportunity to make more of it comes along, we usually take it. Remembering the pain and uncertainties of poverty, we may eagerly sign any long-term contract that guarantees us a steady income. Unfortunately, the contract can lock us into the past, forcing us to labor for yesterday's worries long after they have faded.

A funny thing happens after we have enough of something we lacked: It stops being important. Everyone would love to have a million dollars, but if you had $100 million, would you be 100 times happier? Probably not, because your money problems have already been solved, and your focus is going to turn to other personal issues that aren't related to money. With the extra $99 million you would only buy more things you don't need and probably be burdened by them. It can never make you as happy as the first million did.

This illustrates a recurring problem of human perception. People tend to project recent history into the future in a straight line. For example, if the price of gold has risen dramatically for the past five years, they assume that it is always going to rise, and they buy gold. They don't understand that a past trend is no guarantee of a future one.

Future needs, as they eventually turn out, are rarely a straight-line extrapolation of the present. There is usually a satiation point where the original disequilibrium has been resolved and the trend goes flat or heads in the other direction. The price of gold can't go up dramatically forever. Eventually, it is going to stabilize and probably drop to a more rational and sustainable level.

This "satiation" phenomenon is especially relevant when predicting one's own feelings. If people see that something made them happy in the past, they believe it will always make them happy and that their happiness will be proportional to the supply of that substance. If a million dollars will bring them euphoria, they assume $100 million will give them 100 times the high. They fail to realize that once a need is satiated, it fades into the background, and different needs unexpectedly come to the fore.

When we are romantically unattached, loneliness preoccupies us, just like money did when we were poor. We long to be touched and to have someone care about us. When it finally happens and we find love, our natural inclination is to try to nail down this success with a long-term contract. Remembering how terrible loneliness was, we want to guarantee that it never happens again. Unfortunately, once we commit to a contract, we may discover that it solves only the problems of the past in a straight-line fashion and inhibits us from solving the less predictable problems of the future.

Because your financial assets have been combined, marriage commits you indefinitely to almost daily social interaction with your partner. After your painful loneliness, this seems to be just what the doctor ordered, but after the honeymoon a new concern may loom in your mind: a desire for independence.

What would it be like, you wonder, to wake up in the morning and do anything you wanted without having to negotiate with anyone else? How would it feel to be able to set your own goals and control your own environment? What would you do if you had no one to pick up after or tiptoe around? Wouldn't it be Heaven?

To many married people, this is as wistful and romantic a dream as marriage may seem to those who are single. They lust to be alone! Sociability may be pleasant up to a point, but it is harder to make changes in a team, and you are often held down by the limitations and demands of your teammates. Loneliness is replaced by the tyranny of the group, which often discourages individual achievement. Any group—of two or twenty—tends to operate on a principle of the lowest common denominator, where you only do those few things that everyone can agree on.

In marriage, much of your time is not yours. It is "community property" that can be spent only with permission. If you make a plan for substantial amount of your own time but fail to consult your spouse on it, you could be in trouble. There is often a jealousy thing going on below the surface: "If you spend so much time doing that, you aren't going to have enough time for me!"

After you have done the marriage routine for a while, you may long for a time when you possess no one and no one possesses you. You may secretly dream of going to a luxury hotel on a tropical island and staying there *all alone*. It is the kind of fantasy you keep to yourself, because insecure spouses would never understand. Having an affair is one thing, but wanting to be alone, away from their neediness, is beyond their comprehension.

Some people never get a chance to experience independent living. They move directly from their parents' home, to living with someone, to marriage, to raising children. They never have an opportunity to control their own life. Independence is a great mystery to them, like marriage is to a virgin. "How do you do it?" they ask. They wonder: When you wake up in the morning all alone, how do you decide what to do with your day? Won't you go mad if you don't have sex on a regular basis? Is it safe to live alone? What if you have a stroke or heart attack and no one is there to notice? Aren't you going to die?

Independence is a critical life skill. To accomplish the most you can in your time on Earth, you not only need to get along with others, you also have to get along comfortably with yourself. If you know yourself and what you are capable of, you are probably going to make better decisions for others too. If you don't know yourself, many of your decisions are going to fail because they don't take into account your own limitations.

When they suddenly find themselves alone, many people panic. They turn on the TV, start drinking or engage in some other distracting activity to make the perceived emptiness go away. They lack the skills of independence and self-direction. Without this personal center, they have probably made a lot of bad decisions in their life out of panic and will continue to make them without much self-awareness. Self-awareness usually arises from private meditation and thinking time, and because these people experience little of it, their analysis of their own life does not run very deep.

Comfortable independence is when you find yourself alone and consider it a joy! Now, you can do all those things that other people prevented you from doing. When you are self-directed, you don't panic or waste time. Instead, you try to make the most of your time and you don't let any of it slip away.

To be kept in tune, the skill of independence needs to be practiced on a regular basis—not just once a year but preferably every day. Maybe independence should be your default position, with relationships being only temporary departures for as long as the joy is real or a need is served.

The Seduction of Novelty

Let's say you visit a place of great scenic beauty, like the Rocky Mountains of Montana or the perfect beach on Maui. You are so impressed by the scenery that you decide to make it your own. At great expense, you buy a house with a picture window that looks out on the very scene you adore so much. Now you can possess it forever!

What happens then? After a few days, you stop noticing the scenery. You get used to it, and it stops registering on your consciousness. Instead of thinking about where your house is located, you become preoccupied once again with what is going on inside. In the long run, all that matters is the projects you are working on and the problems you are facing, not the view through the window.

This describes an inherent problem of beauty and all other forms of sensual pleasure. If you find the perfect chocolate cake and surround yourself with it, it is eventually going to lose its appeal. You get the full sensual pleasure from something only when it is new or relatively rare. The more you experience it, the more it turns routine, until it becomes part of the background that you hardly notice.

As enthralled as you may be with your romantic partner right now, the sensual part of your relationship is certain to grow dull after a while. You are going to stop noticing all their fixed characteristics you once found so appealing: the sound of their voice, the color of their eyes, the shape of their body, etc. All you will be concerned with over time is the operational and intellectual part of the relationship—how well you execute projects and solve problems together. The color of their eyes has no bearing.

Drug addicts also notice this phenomenon: Their first high from a new drug is fantastic, the second is almost as good, the third good, the fourth routine, etc. Over time, you have to take more and more of the drug to achieve the same effect, and eventually even that doesn't work. Soon you are taking the drug not for the high it gives you but because of how bad you feel when you do not take it.

In psychological terms, this process is called "adjustment." Whatever new experience you encounter, good or bad, your brain is eventually going to adjust to it and the experience will come to seem normal and routine. The sensual passions of the experience are destined to fade, and what you have left are the practical problems of living.

It would be great to win millions in a lottery. The experience would be exciting at first, and it might seem that all your problems are solved. Even that good fortune, however, will eventually seem routine. Yes, some of your problems will be solved, but you will find they are replaced by a whole new set of problems—probably ones that money can't fix. No matter what happens to you, good or bad, you will adjust to it and your overall happiness will probably drift back to the same level as before.

Most people seem to have great difficulty grasping the concept of adjustment and predicting it in their own lives. They think that if they are attracted to something new right now, they are going to be attracted to it forever, and they may have no problem signing a long-term contract guaranteeing its permanent delivery.

If you are in love with a certain kind of chocolate cake,

and someone offers you a special discount, you might eagerly sign a contract to have this cake delivered to you every week for the rest of your life. What you are bound to discover, however, is the company changes the recipe. Your fourth and fifth delivered cake does not taste nearly as good as the first. You call up the company to angrily complain, but they assure you that, no, the recipe has not changed. Only your brain has.

People are easily seduced by novelty. They'll buy whatever the new thing is—like the latest entertainment device—without realizing how quickly it will become the old thing. They are even willing to go into debt to buy the new thing, so they are still paying for it even after it has become obsolete.

If a certain product thrills you now, then you figure the same product ought to thrill you just as much tomorrow and the day after. If the product still has the same ingredients and physical characteristics, science suggests that it should produce the same emotional reaction every time. But the brain doesn't work that way. Most pleasure depends on novelty. You laugh at a joke, for example, only because it is new—because it blazes a new neurological trail through your brain. You might laugh at the joke the second time you hear it, but probably not the third, fourth and fifth. It has lost its novelty and thus its pleasure.

When we encounter a new experience that appeals to us, we tend to repeat it. If we like a movie, we may be drawn back to see it again and again. There is a limit, however, to how many times we will do this. Sooner or later, our brain has explored every nuance of the experience and will be ready to move on.

Of course, you can't move on if you have already signed a long-term contract committing you to that experience. Then you may be forced to repeat it long after you have lost your passion. In that case, real pleasure is eventually replaced by the intellectualization of pleasure, where you say the same words and claim the same passion but don't feel the same feelings inside.

How many exciting new products have you bought and used only once? If you have a garage, it is probably filled with these failed experiments. You were swept away be the novelty of the product, but once you had it in your hands your passion faded quickly. You don't use the product now because it turned out not to fit your practical operational lifestyle. What you are left with is the dull carcass of a dream, occupying space in your garage. You can't bear to throw it away because you spent so much on it, but it just doesn't work for you anymore.

Life, after a while, can become an accumulation of these dead dreams. You repeat the same old activities, thinking that they must be pleasurable because they once were, but you don't feel the same feelings. You only tell yourself you do because you have already invested so much.

Only wisdom and freedom can keep your life vibrant. Wisdom is the ability to recognize when your own feelings have changed, and freedom is the ability to move on to something new. Long-term contracts tend to suppress both. You insist that your feelings remain the same because change is not a realistic option.

That's why nearly everyone engaged in a lifelong contract claims to be happy with it. Maybe the chocolate cake your ordered years ago tastes flat in your mouth, but you have to believe you made the right choice because the alternatives are just too painful to bear.

The Investment Effect

"I love this place and wouldn't want to live anywhere else."

You hear this from established middle-aged people in every part of the world. From the lochs of Scotland to the deserts of Arizona, as long as someone is feeling no great pain in their habitat, they will probably claim to love it there. On the coast of British Columbia, local residents say they love the ocean, forests and mountains. In Manhattan, they love their hypothetical cultural life and how their city "never sleeps." In Massachusetts, people say they love their four seasons and their rich variety of weather.

It is pretty much the same when people talk about their own marriage: "I wouldn't have wanted it any other way!" You hear these sentimental words especially on anniversaries, Valentine's Day and other occasions when sentiment is called for. Is this evidence that their marriage is a success and we should follow these happy people down the same path? Not necessarily. *Anyone* who has made a big lifetime investment is going to claim it was the right one.

I grew up in Massachusetts but am not impressed with the "four seasons" claim. I say the weather there is horrible! Rain then snow then slush then drizzle. It is a burden on the quality of life and makes everything harder. I find Massachusetts pleasant to visit in June, but I would never want to move back there year-round. What makes me different from the people who live in Massachusetts and say they love the change of seasons? I am no longer invested there.

If you have bought real estate in a certain place and established a life there, of course you are going to love it. You have to! But which comes first: Are you living there because you love it, or do you love this place because you live there and not claiming to love it would be a painful reflection on your past choices and outstanding investments?

Whenever people extol the virtues of something they have already invested in and try to convince you to join them, you ought to be suspicious. By selling the same lifestyle to you, they are trying to justifying their own past decisions. Their love for this lifestyle may be real to them, but it is also self-serving. It helps them avoid unpleasant thoughts and painful dilemmas.

If you come to a fork in the road at an early stage of your life and you choose one path over another, then the farther down that path you go, the more you will probably declare your love for your choice. "This path is the best!" you say, even if you have no experience with any other. "I wouldn't want to have gone any other way!"

You are especially going to believe in your choice if it was very costly one. If you had to wade through swamps and wrestle alligators to get where you are today, it only increases your love for your current path. The greater the sacrifice you have already made, the more you have to believe in your current itinerary to avoid suffering painful regrets.

If you invest in one path and are less than successful at it than you hoped, your natural inclination is to invest even more in that same path rather than turning back. Why? Because you need to justify the expensive investment you have already made. It is like sitting in front of a slot machine and losing $1000. The more you have lost, the more you feel compelled to keep gambling to try to recoup those losses. In some way, you figure that machine owes you a reward for your sacrifice.

In fact, every spin of the reels on a slot machine is entirely random. The fact that you have already lost $1000 has no bearing at all on the next spin. The machine doesn't "owe" you anything, but gamblers instinctively believe that it does. The more they sacrifice, the more they believe in their machine and that a big win is just around the corner.

I call this phenomenon "Investment Bias." (Psychologists call it the "Sunk Cost Fallacy.") This is the tendency of a prior investment to increase your emotional attachment to the path you have already chosen. Your prior investment encourages you to select and distort the available evidence to favor the underlying beliefs supporting the investment.

What do married couples say on their 25th wedding anniversary? "Dear, if I had it to do all over again, I wouldn't want to change a thing!" Of course they're going to say that! They have already invested 25 years in this arrangement— probably most of their adult lives. They are not likely to turn back now and say, "Oops, made a mistake!"

I'm not saying their love isn't genuinely felt on both sides, but unless they are truly free to leave each other, it is mandatory love, not quite the same as the free-will kind they had at the beginning.

The fact that people married 25 years still say they love each other shouldn't be taken as evidence in support of the institution of marriage. A young person might say, "Look how happy they are!" and claim this as justification for their own marriage. Unfortunately, claimed love and happiness aren't really the issue, because anyone can make themselves believe in their past choice. The real question is how productive the relationship has been compared to the potential alternatives that were locked out.

How do you define "productive"? That's something for you

to decide. Surely, there must be things you want to accomplish before you die. Your life must have some purpose other than just procreating and avoiding pain. Is your only purpose on Earth to repeat the lives of your elders? If you expect to accomplish something more, then your relationship can be judged productive if it serves that mission better than any other available road.

Sentiment in marriage often sounds like a religious believer's explanation of his beliefs: circular arguments that are unfathomable to an outsider. "I wouldn't have wanted to marry anyone else," they say, but they haven't had a chance to experience anyone else so how do they really know? Faith mainly—if not faith in God then faith in some other magical force that drew the two of them together.

Every couple has a "Genesis Story" about how that met and fell in love. If your parents were married, you probably heard their story many times—how Dad fell in love with Mom the moment he lay eyes on her, etc. The story always has a certain fairytale quality to it, as though angels had ordained this romance. Kinda makes you want to know what *really* happened, since no romance in the real world ever seems to come close.

If you have been chained together with someone for 25 years, and you put those chains on willingly, you have to believe in your choice. You have to create a mythology that supports your earlier decision. That doesn't mean that your choice really was the best, only that you have to believe in it.

Back to the Sixties

"All You Need is Love," sang the Beatles in 1967. The song went instantly to #1 on the pop music charts and has poisoned our thinking about love ever since.

Love is *not* all you need. There are countless problems it can't solve. Love can be a powerful drug that makes you *think* it's all you need, but sooner or later you have to come up for air and deal with all the problems love encouraged you to put off.

Love won't put food on the table or solve your financial problems. It also won't give your life purpose and meaning, at least in the long run. There will be a period of infatuation when you will be satisfied just exploring each other, but eventually every nook and cranny has been plumbed and you're back where you were before: "What do I do now?"

It's like landing on a fascinating little island with a castle and a quaint fishing village on it. You can spend many days exploring the island, but pretty soon you've mastered it, and everything there becomes routine. That's when it dawns on you: You're on an *island*, and there's no place else to go. Love might land you on this island, but love won't get you off.

Love does give you a default plan. Kids of my era taunted each other with this verse: "First comes love, then comes marriage, then comes Johnny with a baby carriage." It has been the default plan for generations, and it doesn't show any signs of losing steam, but is it the best plan for you?

If you don't take the baby route, then what do you do with yourself? If you didn't know who you were before you fell in love, and your partner didn't know who they were, then why would a relationship give you any more direction? Now you are *two* people who don't know what to do with their lives, except now you both have to agree on whatever plan you come up with.

When two teenagers fall in love and run away together, what do they do? They drive around, go to the city, scrounge for food and gas money, drive some more, sleep in the car, have sex to exhaustion, start arguing with each other, then eventually give up and go home. Love, they usually find the hard way, isn't "all you need."

It was irresponsible for the Beatles to claim it was.

The late Sixties were the era of Free Love. Contraception became widely available for the first time and spawned the Sexual Revolution. Sex finally came out of the closet, was discussed openly and practiced prodigiously. Love became "free" for a while, but it didn't stay that way. Eventually reality caught up.

It is fine for flower children to copulate like bunnies, but the age-old question remains: What do you do next? It may be exhilarating to explore your sexuality, but the thrill can't last. Once you've experienced all of the Kama Sutra positions, it becomes like the chocolate cake you've eaten too much of: It just doesn't give you the same excitement anymore. Instead, you're soon back to the same problems of living you had before, except now you have more baggage.

The Sexual Revolution was eventually perverted by pornographers and tainted by venereal diseases. Free Love got shut down pretty quickly, and a new equilibrium developed that we know today. You could call it "Pay-Per-View Love." Sex was freed from the subscription plan of marriage. Couples could now enjoy carnal knowledge out of wedlock without it being considered a crime or even improper, and a child could be born out of wedlock without being called a "bastard." Thus, marriage lost its significance as a real transition between life stages.

Before the Sixties, marriage was a necessary gateway to sex and the legitimacy of your children. After the Sixties, it was an optional step taken chiefly for emotional purposes. Marriage didn't lose its popularity, however. Turns out, people still wanted the ceremony, even if it had little practical significance apart from finances.

People seem to have a powerful need for ceremonies. When someone dies, for example, their friends and family feel a need to get together to say a few words. It doesn't matter what the ceremony consists of. You could say "ashes to ashes" or "So long, Bro!" or anything else. What people seem to crave is official public recognition of a transitional event. People need a funeral so they can say definitively, "He's gone," and begin moving on with their lives.

Most couples don't seem satisfied to just be secure in their own relationship, for itself by itself. They want public recognition that their relationship exists. The wedding ceremony seems to provide that. It is a sort of public notarization service, witnessed by everyone the couple knows, so buddies of the groom can finally say, "He's gone."

The modern wedding ceremony is composed of an accumulation of traditions dating to the Romans and before. This often includes contributions by Lennon and McCartney, who have become part of our romantic tradition as much as Romeo and Juliet. Whereas pre-Sixties weddings pretty much stuck to the traditional religiously mandated script and emphasized duty and responsibility, post-Sixties weddings began to go free-form, and you never knew what would happen before or after "I do."

Modern weddings are all about expressing love in unique ways so it doesn't seem like the couple is forming a financial institution (which they are). These days, you are supposed to customize your wedding so it seems uniquely yours. The ceremony is all "love" this and "cherish" that, going light on the "duty" and very light on the "death do you part" part (which is now commonly transliterated as "as long as you both shall live" or the more realistic "from this day forth"). She looks into his eyes and he looks into hers, and they recite the carefully selected magic words they have been sweating over for months.

Some older members of the audience, however, are squirming in their seats, knowing full well how corny this is going to look in the wedding video when viewed ten years from now. By then, statistics suggest, the marriage will probably be Splitsville and the video will become one of those youthful embarrassments best forgotten.

We can only hope someone has the good sense to delete it from YouTube.

When Love Ends but the Marriage Doesn't

A large portion of marriages end in divorce, but that does not mean that the remaining marriages—the ones that seem to last for life—are a success. Divorce is just the easiest failure to measure, since it is a publically recorded legal event. There are no statistics to tell you about marriages that have failed by any emotional or practical measure but that continue on in name.

We could call them "nominal marriages." I became aware of one kind of nominal marriage when I ran into an old friend. She said her marriage has been loveless for five years, but she has no plans to file for divorce. Both parties recognize their affection is gone, but they continue to reside in the same house to care for their two children.

Like college roommates, their relationship is defined by clear boundaries. She has her part of the house; he has his. He has control of the kids in the evenings and on Saturdays; she has them in the afternoons and Sundays. When they pass, they are civil to each other, as roommates might be who have little in common, but they make no attempt to share their emotions.

None of this arrangement is in writing, and few outside the household know about it. It is just what has been worked out. Both parties regard divorce as too expensive, both to their finances and to their children. They lead separate lives in the same house, and the arrangement seems stable, even if not warm.

This seemingly bizarre relationship is probably more common than the rest of us would guess. The statistics for divorce are clear, but there is no way to quantify when love has died without divorce. Maybe this represents only a tiny fraction of marriages or maybe it is the dominant form. No one knows but the parties themselves.

Many a politician has been seen in solidarity with their spouse on the campaign trail only to be divorced shortly after the election. When this happens, one wonders if the love they displayed on camera was real. You begin to question the love of all public marriages. Is this love genuinely felt or a display for political gain?

Likewise, you see a couple—married or unmarried—who you think look so happy together. "I want a love like that!" you say. It is with some shock that you find them breaking up a short time later, each with a litany of festering complaints you never suspected. It makes you wonder how many marriages are truly happy.

There are so many kinds of dysfunctional marriage that you can't even begin to quantify them. The health of a marriage has little to do with how happy people claim to be. The success of any life choice can only be judged against what could have been. As long as you never think about these possibilities, every marriage is a success.

A loveless marriage can stay together for political or religious reasons or purely practical ones. Many couples have built a financial empire together under the umbrella of the marital community, and dividing it up might seem too costly. Divorce is nothing if not expensive! Others might not be able to afford two homes. Staying together "for the children" is another excuse for an unhealthy marriage to drag on, although you wonder how well the children are really served when their parents in the same home don't get along.

Of the long-term marriages you've seen at close range, how many do you regard as truly successful? If you choose to look closely, you see some serious dysfunction in most. Truly egalitarian ones seem outnumbered by those where one partner has devolved into a child-like state and the other becomes the parent. The protector may know that love has died but he/she maintains the status quo out of a sense of duty, in memory of those ancient wedding vows.

Can a loveless marriage be healthy? Is it truly best for the children? That depends on the alternatives, if any. Life is full of imperfect solutions dictated by circumstances that are now beyond our control. Still, such an arrangement has to be confining to both parties. A stagnant relationship can be a prison, discouraging to personal growth, because the established boundaries are so hard to change.

To be truly single again, truly whole and responsible, both parties have to control their own finances and destiny. Even if living in peace with your erstwhile partner, you're a fly trapped in amber, a Sleeping Beauty, until the spell is somehow broken. Divorce can help you with that! As much as we regard divorce as a failure, it can be the only relief from an even worse hell. The only thing worse than divorce is a failed marriage that does not end. Like bankruptcy, divorce is a chance to back away from your previous mistakes, wipe the slate clean and start over.

To the currently unmarried, the lesson is: Just because "everyone" is married doesn't mean every marriage is happy. An undetermined number of those marriages are not working, and the probable success of any one marriage may be bleaker than even the divorce statistics suggest.

Trapped in their own Museum

The legal contract of marriage is chiefly a financial one, merging the economies of two individuals into one undifferentiated community. This may not seem too dangerous at first, but marriage is usually only the beginning. What happens next can be truly terrifying: real estate!

If the couple has the means to do so, they will soon buy a home together. Typically, they will be agreeing to a mortgage of 20-30 years. It is this mutual commitment, perhaps more than the marriage itself, that begins to lock them into place like mammoths trapped in tar.

Once they have a seemingly permanent home, what do they do next? They start filling it with stuff! I mean STUFF, piles and piles of it, most of which they don't really need. The home and contents therein becomes an outward expression of their romantic oneness. The stuff they acquire is largely aesthetic in nature. It is suppose to convey who they are, individually and as a community.

Humans have always been natural pack rats. The storage of both food and tools has been essential to mankind's survival for most of its history. In the modern world, the same impulse is mostly dysfunctional, just like our craving for fat and sugar. As a rule, whenever people have space for stuff they will fill it with stuff. Nothing that might theoretically be useful in the future can ever be thrown away. No wall can be left blank, and every aesthetic sense must be catered to. Any unused floor space will eventually be filled with something useless, until the entire living space is stuffed with stuff and the couple starts looking for larger quarters.

Individuals collect stuff, too, but rarely to the degree that married couples do. This is due in part to bureaucratic inefficiency: Nothing can be thrown away unless both agree. If one partner uses less than half of the available storage space, the other will probably fill it up for them. As in all things, the discipline of the couple together is rarely better than the discipline of the weakest partner.

Legally, a wedding heralds a new financial arrangement, while socially and psychologically, it declares to others the supposed strength of a couple's bond. Commercially, however, a wedding is an important launching point for economic activity. It is the start of a massive movement of furniture, art objects, consumer goods and maintenance services into a newly opened market.

Getting married is usually the beginning of the Great Accumulation.

Since the couple has supposedly "arrived" at a permanent plateau of stability, they feel more comfortable accumulating things. The collecting of merchandise is also a bonding activity, since even if the couple has nothing in common intellectually they can still go shopping together.

A wedding is usually a prelude to interior decoration, at least in the short term. In the long term, it is a prelude to a garage sale, a big one, where all that useless stuff is finally sold off at a tiny fraction of what the couple paid for it. The garage sale usually happens at the time of the divorce or when both partners drop dead and their heirs are forced to get rid of it for them.

Stuff is a substantial part of the substance of marriage. In the absence of children, marriage consists largely of acquiring stuff, rearranging stuff ("Honey, can you help me move this?"), maintaining and caring for the stuff you have (including the home itself and any pets and plants therein) and eventually the contentious division of stuff at the time of divorce.

Is this all life consists of—stuff?

Some couples live in trash heaps of stuff, but the highest ideal of marriage is to live in a pristine museum, surrounded by objects of sentimental value and artistic merit that radiate good taste. Everything you have done or accomplished should be placed on display: your diplomas, photos of you at important times of your life, mementos of every vacation you and your spouse have taken and visual documentation of your entire genetic lineage. It would be difficult to get a public museum to put together a display like this unless you happen to be very famous. If you own the display space, however, you can do anything you want with it.

Once they have reached the plateau of marriage, couples with the means usually set about creating a shrine to themselves. They consult with each other on what the shrine will look like and the objects that will be included in it. "Do you think this painting looks better on this wall or that one?" Every object is seen as an expression of who they are, who they were or who they want to be.

It is a never ending project! Once the museum seems finished, the completion date can be endlessly extended by a process called "remodeling," where you tear things down only to rebuild them. Shouldn't we add a sun room out back? Don't we need to rearrange the flower garden? Shouldn't we turn the basement into an entertainment center? As long as funds are available, work on the museum can continue indefinitely.

It certainly looks like there is a relationship going on. The couple is working together toward common a goal: interior decoration. They are getting along with each other, and they have plenty of things to talk about—mainly their current and future remodeling. They conduct research together, including reviewing the religious works of Martha Stewart and Bob Vila. They travel together—to Home Depot and the plant nursery. It looks like they are living a full and productive matrimonial existence.

But are they?

Marriage seems like a step forward from selfish isolation. No longer will you be preoccupied only with yourself; now you will be sharing everything you have with another. You have found your "other half" so you no longer have to be lonely. You give to them and they give to you, so you no longer seem so self-absorbed.

But what do we call it when someone builds a shrine to themselves, when they are occupied only with their own needs and when they cut themselves off from the needs of the outside world? Isn't this "narcissism"—an unhealthy preoccupation with oneself?

In this case, however, the narcissism is shared by two. They may be generous or selfless with each other, but if they are sharing little with the outside world they are still self-absorbed. Any resources devoted to the shrine obviously can't be spent on anything else. By reinforcing each other's self-serving delusions, they may be cutting themselves off from any real accomplishment.

Once you have created the perfect museum and a comprehensive shrine to everything you are, what happens to it? Eventually, you die; the museum is disassembled and the home and its contents are sold to strangers. Most of your life's work is translated into filthy lucre, which is split among your heirs.

As tasteful as the museum might have once been, there is nothing left to remember you by. There is nothing lasting you have accomplished. You have just remodeled the house again and again and gained nothing from it in the long run.

In the modern world, the substance of marriage seems to be mainly product acquisition and interior decoration. When you run out of other things in common, you can still renovate, but is that all you were meant to do with your life?

Problems of Living

By virtue of being human, all of us are driven by recurring existential urges. These are deep emotional fears, similar to hunger and thirst, that secretly motivate our behavior and sometimes lead us to ruin. Our existential desires are not always fulfillable and are often self-contradictory, yet we have to learn to live with them.

One of these essential drives is the desire to be protected, comforted and cared for—call it the "urge to merge." Most of us remember warm feelings of security from our childhood: Our parents took care of our needs, comforted us when we were hurt and protected us from the harsh realities of the world. With time, we chafed under this protection and wanted to experience the world more directly. This was thrilling at first until we realized how cruel and unforgiving the real world can be. When reality didn't go our way, we longed to go back to being protected. We wanted to fall back into someone else's arms and feel comforted and safe again.

Alas, you can never really go back. Every form of refuge has its price, and even if you pay the price, any protection may still be an illusion.

People join religions for the illusion of protection. A religion gives you a set of comforting words to say and rituals to follow, and it teaches you about a God or other supernatural force that is supposedly looking after you. The only trouble with religion is that it compromises your own independent judgment. If you follow the simplistic instructions of the group rather than judging life on its own terms, this is bound to lead to painful real-world mistakes.

With almost the same religious fervor, people look to romantic love as a source of protection. They want their partner to be a parent to them, even a god. They want to be held in someone's arms and be kept warm and safe for the rest of their lives. They want a magical White Knight to rescue them.

Our longing for rescue and belief in White Knights can run deep, so much so that we are tempted to see a rescuer in any mannequin or scarecrow. In the early stages of romance, we worship our partner, seeing them as a Superman or Superwoman with extraordinary abilities, even if we have never actually seen those abilities in action. We need them to have superhuman powers so they can fulfill all of the impossible needs within us.

The comfort, of course, is illusory. Someone can hold us in their arms and tell us comforting words, just like our parents did, but they can't really protect us from reality. Eventually, our protector turns out not to be superhuman. Because they don't know our needs as well as we do they inevitably make worse decisions for us than we would make ourselves, and this may get us into even deeper difficulties than the ones we wanted protection from.

Another existential urge is almost the opposite: the desire to be a unique and powerful individual in our own right. This is what drives us away from the protection of our parents beginning at a very early age. As soon as we have the capability of doing something, like walking, then we want to do it ourselves, without any help from anyone. This need becomes especially fierce in adolescence, when we are desperate for a unique identity and insist that we need help from no one.

Young people will go to some bizarre extremes to try to

prove their uniqueness, like tattooing, body piercing, a taste for loud music their parents hate and a penchant for high-risk activities. Give them a cultural restriction and they'll rebel against it! Unfortunately, this is only shallow theatrical uniqueness. It is not what they really want and need, which is real accomplishment in the outside world.

Paradoxically, we not only want to be unique and powerful, we want to be *seen* as unique and powerful by others. Being independent and self-sufficient isn't usually enough for us, because this is a very lonely position. We want others to see our independence and self-sufficiency. We want to be praised for our uniqueness, and barring that, we will settle for being reviled for it. The important thing is that we be noticed. We want to make a mark on the world. We want to prove to others that we exist.

Everyone wants witnesses, preferably a million of them, but even one witness is better than not being seen at all. We feel more alive when we know someone is watching us and recording our accomplishments. In our childhood, our parents provided this service: When we achieved something, they praised us for it. When we said, "Mommy, look at me!" she looked and said encouraging words.

In adulthood, we also want this praise and notice. We work hard in our careers not just for money but for recognition. Being the Number One sales agent in your corporate division gives you a sense of worth deeper than money, because everyone else in your local tribe is now recognizing you.

If a tree falls in the forest and there is no one to see, does it still fall? Physically, it does, but emotionally maybe not. If you have accomplished something, and no one is there to see your accomplishment, then is it worth anything? There may be some private satisfaction in, say, climbing the world's highest mountain, but public recognition for it feels much better.

Romance is also supposed to fulfill this need. No longer will your accomplishments go unnoticed. Your partner will praise you just as your parents did. They will see and mentally record everything you do, which may give you a greater sense of having done it. The more powerful we make our witnesses out to be, the more valuable the recognition.

This is sometimes a hollow recognition. If your partner praises everything you do regardless of its quality, then their notice won't mean much. On the other hand, your accomplishment could be taken for granted after a while and not praised at all, to the point where you are making great efforts in the relationship and getting little recognition. If you are trapped with someone in a fixed relationship, either result is possible. One way or another, the witnessing of the other person loses its value.

Why should it matter whether we have a witness? If we accomplish a personal goal, shouldn't the accomplishment alone be satisfaction enough without the need for an audience? Being witnessed matters because we are essentially social beings. How others see us forms part of our identity and our core motivation. We couldn't just arrive on an alien planet and know what to do with ourselves. The people around us necessarily mold us and direct us toward certain goals, and without any human contact at all we would be lost.

We can be self-sufficient to a degree, but there could be no worse hell than being trapped on a desert island alone. Without someone to perform for, the theatre of life begins to lose its meaning. If you see another human face only once a year, that contact is still essential to keep you going. Even the *dream* of human contact is better than no contact at all.

The existential drives may not always make logical sense, but they will always be part of us. We will always be seeking comfort and recognition from others at the same time we are trying to separate ourselves from them. It is okay to fall into the arms of another and to seek fame and recognition for your specialness, but you can't suspend reality in the process.

Whatever you are seeking emotionally, you need to choose a path that is really going to give you what you want. Your quest must be moderated by intelligence. For example, joining a religious cult is not the best way to seek comfort and personal affirmation. Likewise, you shouldn't pursue a path toward fame and fortune that isn't really going to lead to satisfaction. You can try to become a movie star, but it probably won't make you happy even if you succeed. Real emotional satisfaction generally requires real accomplishment, not the public illusion of accomplishment.

You can't ignore your existential urges, but you must handle them with discipline, like a parent managing their children. For their own good, your feelings can't be allowed to do whatever they want. Having a need, dictated by emotions, does not mean that blindly obeying your emotions will get that need fulfilled.

If you are cautious, thoughtful and open to the unexpected, you might find enough comfort, uniqueness and recognition to get you by. You probably won't find them, however, if you simply lock yourself in a prison cell with a captive audience and throw away the key.

Lifelong Learning

Childhood is a period of intense intellectual and emotional development. The child must learn how to function in a strange body on an alien planet among a family he didn't choose. He has to learn a spoken language from scratch, and he does it much faster than an adult ever could. Every day, he absorbs new things and becomes more in tune with his environment. When the child is old enough, he is sent to school, where new skills are built upon previously learned ones. Primary school is followed by secondary school and possibly by college and grad school. Ideally, he learns a professional skill, becomes proficient at it, then settles into an adult career.

What happens then? In most cases, his learning slows to a crawl.

Between the ages of 5 and 15, the developmental changes are huge. A personality and a physical body are formed which will probably remain stable for the person's lifetime. Between 15 and 25, there can still be major personal changes as formal education is completed and a person settles into an initial career path. Between 25 and 35, the changes are less significant. Unless a person has been the victim of misfortune, like war or layoffs, their growth tends to be only incremental. They advance further along their previously chosen career path but don't usually deviate much into new areas.

Between 35 and 45, personal growth may be imperceptible from the outside. If you leave one of your former classmates and come back to visit them ten years later, you usually find they have more gray hair and have stabilized in their social role, but compared to their younger selves it usually looks like they have been held in suspended animation, with little obvious personal growth.

In general, people don't change much between that point and death. The body slowly deteriorates and the mind becomes set in its ways. As a rule, older people tend to be more interested in comfort than change.

Is this our destiny? Does the brain simply lose its ability to learn after the first few years? Or is this a choice? Do people stop developing simply because they have decided it is no longer a priority?

A young child learns a new language effortlessly. If he is exposed to three languages in his infancy, he will learn all three without an accent and without much formal training. An adult could never do that. The person who grew up with only one language usually has to struggle for years to learn a new one, and even then he will probably never grasp it as intuitively as the child. Does this mean the adult's brain has slowed down and is no longer capable of significant learning?

Not necessarily. The adult is usually trying to learn a language part time, while the infant is devoted continuously to the task. If you kidnapped an adult and threw him together with a caring and patient family in a foreign land where he had to use local words to get what he wanted, he would probably learn as fast as the child does. The structure of the brain no doubt changes between infancy and adulthood, but the raw ability to learn is still present. The child learns by listening for the music while the adult learns by discovering rules. Each method has its advantages, but neither is inherently superior.

Adults do not lose their ability to learn; they just do it in different ways. If an adult decides tomorrow he is fascinated by a new technology and wants to learn everything he can about it, he will do it on his own, probably more efficiently than the child because he has more intellectual tools at his disposal. The only problem is getting the adult motivated to learn at all.

Between childhood and adulthood the emotional circumstances change. A young child is committed to nothing and is not expected to produce anything valuable to others. He can decide one day he wants to be a firefighter and the next day a nurse. He can experiment with a lot of different viewpoints without being tied to any one. His schooling sets up a graduated series of structured challenges, so he is required to learn every day. He develops rapidly because his environment makes it easy for him to do so.

Adults, however, tend to get trapped by their commitments and stuck in repetitive routines. They reach "plateaus" where no further learning is expected of them and where the circumstances of their life actively discourage change. Once an adult has invested in a certain way of life, unregulated learning becomes downright dangerous because it might lead him in directions other than what he has already invested in. To protect himself emotionally, he tends to repeat the same comfortable activities over and over—bowling every Wednesday night, fishing on weekends, etc.—because these reliable patterns insulate him and do not threatened his investments.

Without the physical and emotional freedom to explore and experiment, learning becomes much less likely. For example, to learn about a new country, you have to actually go there, not just watch it on TV. If you are trapped in any kind of prison, your personal development is bound to slow, not because your brain has solidified but because your range of possible real-world experiments is now so limited.

College students with few commitments can easily learn about a foreign country: They just grab their backpack and go! Married people with mortgages and children can't do this. They are limited to their 2-week annual vacation, and then they need someone to take care of their kids, pets, lawn and prior commitments. Given their accumulated habits and their established status, backpacking probably isn't good enough for them. They must have a fine hotel! Their trip will probably end up being a big, expensive production. If it happens at all, it will probably be far less efficient and educational than the college student's.

Intelligence is not an innate talent but a choice. Some adults are smart and others stupid mainly because they choose to be and arrange their lives that way. Smart people remain so because they deliberately seek out new experiences and are actively experimenting with new ideas. They have also set up their life in such a way as to accommodate the unpredictability of their own development. Dumb people repeat the same ritualized activities over and over and allow their practical commitments to expand to the point where no further change is possible. Henceforth, they do not learn or grow very much unless change is forced upon them.

If you are going to grow as much in your later years as you did in your early ones, you have to make a conscious decision to do so and arrange your life accordingly. You have to adopt an attitude that unplanned change is desirable and be willing to limit your current worldly commitments to make it possible.

Romantic love may be compatible with learning as long as it is flexible and modifiable. A lifetime contract is not compatible with growth. If you want to develop beyond the state you are currently in, then you have to leave yourself the ability to change in ways you cannot now predict.

Personal Development

All of us should be growing, learning and changing throughout our lives, right? The person we will be ten years from now ought to be significantly wiser and more mature than the person we are today. If you look back at yourself ten years ago, weren't you hopelessly naïve back then? A decade from now, you will probably look back on today's you and think the same thing, Today's you will always be a teenager to tomorrow's you, so it is not wise to give the current you too much power.

Growth is natural and healthy, and we ought to be planning for it. You can't predict how you will change, but you can at least leave open the possibility of it. You cannot grow if you think you have life all worked out in the beginning and leave yourself no other options. True growth implies that whatever your original plans may be, you are going to deviate from them.

You encourage growth not by nailing down a rigid plan but by leaving yourself as many future options as possible. Instead of making plans, you build skills. Don't decide what to do at a fork until you actually reach it. In the meantime, you work on your toolbox, making sure you have plenty of skills and a spectrum of options when those forks come along.

Because it deprives you of the freedom to deviate, marriage tends to freeze your personal development at the state it was at on your wedding day. If your marriage is "successful," by the measures you declared, you will be pretty much the same person ten years from now as you are today. Marriage assumes a steady-state condition: You are so confident of your current path that you are locking yourself into it permanently.

In marriage, anything unusual you do has to be negotiated with your partner. That means you have to put all anticipated changes into words in the required format and submit them explicitly for consideration. Then you have to go through the expensive political process of achieving a consensus. You can't just wake up with a good idea and do it. There's a bureaucracy you have to deal with.

And you shouldn't think that just because your spouse says, "Okay," that your proposal has actually been approved. Surface approval does not imply subterranean compliance. Even if your spouse agrees verbally to something or doesn't raise a protest, there still may be grudges and grievances building up below the surface. No matter how cooperative the two of you seem to be, there is always a power struggle going on behind the scenes, and eventually it is going to erupt into the open.

You have probably learned from previous eruptions that it is best not to rock the boat if you don't have to. Successful couples tend to find a comfortable routine and stick with it. Every morning, they wake up and go through the same rituals and motions. The less deviation there is, the less there is a possibility of conflict.

People who are about to get married typically point to some older couple as their inspiration. Betty and John Smith have been married 50 years—don't they look happy? Well, yeah, but here is something else that is usually true about Betty and John: There has been very little change in those 50 years. They've probably lived in the same house for most of their marriage. They each have their hobbies that have been set in stone since the beginning of time. The only significant changes in the relationship have been forced from the outside, like economic hardship, illness or the deaths of family members.

A long-term marriage is not a vehicle of growth. At best, it is a vehicle of repetitive stability, which is often the enemy of growth. If you are going to hold out Betty and John as an example of what you are working toward, you also have to ask yourself: "Do I want to be doing the same things for 50 years?" It may be fine for Betty and John—both the product of an earlier era—but is it right for you?

The critical thing about Betty and John that made their marriage last is they don't have huge expectations. They expect each new day to be the same as the last. Modern young people, however, demand change. They expect "excitement" in their relationship at the same time they want "stability"— with no clear plan of how they are going to reconcile the two. There is no way you can expect excitement if you have been living with someone for years, because you already know all their tricks. The most you can expect is a sort of comfortable sibling relationship were there are no surprises. Is this really what you are hoping for?

To support the highest level of personal growth, you have to have the ability to entirely change your lifestyle on relatively short notice. You can't expect real personal growth and still keep your nice house in the suburbs with two cars, three cats, a garden and all the attached anchorage. It may be a velvet prison, but it is still a prison. Within a prison, you can still be learning: You can learn how to better deal with your imprisonment. That's not the same, however, as really being able to explore the world.

If a unique opportunity arises tomorrow to do something you never anticipated and you are able to jump on it immediately, then you will experience real creative and intellectual growth, especially if things do *not* go according to plan. If you are free, every disaster is a new opportunity for self-education. As an adult, there is no reason you can't grow as much as young people do when they move away to college, but only if you are prepared to make big changes on short notice. If an opportunity arises and you can't jump on it because you are committed to a preexisting plan, then you will not grow very much. You will remain in stasis.

Every relationship is a trade-off between freedom and engagement. To sustain any relationship, you have to surrender some of your independence and some of your ability to change. The services you get in return may be worth it. It isn't necessarily true, however, that by giving up more of your freedom you are getting more in return. The returns diminish if you commit yourself too much to a relationship at the cost of your own growth.

Certainly, you have to give up a lot of your own potential if you commit yourself to raising children. In that case, however, it can be said that you are transferring some of your own freedom and potential to them. Hopefully, your sacrifice is an investment in their future and the future of society. A romantic relationship is not the same kind of investment. Your partner has already grown to adulthood and is pretty much set in their ways. It is hard to say that your sacrifice to them is going to improve the future of humanity.

Raising children is a unilateral engagement: You will do your best for them regardless of whether you are directly rewarded for it. A romantic relationship, on the other hand, is more like a mutual business arrangement, where real current benefit is expected on both sides. In romance, you *should* expect to be rewarded for any compromise or sacrifice you make, and relatively quickly. If the relationship is not beneficial to you personally—greater than the energy you are expending on it— then it simply needs to end. It is not your responsibility to be the parent to another adult.

It may sound greedy and selfish, but you should be involved in romance mainly for one thing: as a tool for your own growth. For this growth to happen, the relationship has to remain dynamic and alive and to a certain extent dangerous and uncertain. "Security" and a dynamic and growing relationship are simply incompatible.

In a dynamic relationship, there must always be the possibility that you will break up tomorrow. You stay together for the sole reason that the relationship works and is better for you than any other. If this isn't true, then it means you are trapped and your own growth will slow to a crawl.

Social Pressure

Like it or not, we are all part of a network of relationships we did not choose. Our parents, relatives and neighbors were handed to us at birth. The assignment was not fair or rational, just the luck of the draw. Our family formed us until we were strong enough to start forming ourselves; after that they became as much a burden as an asset. We love them, no doubt, but our elders can be intrusive and demanding at times. They made choices about their own lives, implied in our upbringing, and inevitably they want us to follow in their footsteps.

Anyone trapped in a prison of their own making usually wants you to join them. The more they have sacrificed, the more they want others to make the same sacrifices to affirm the wisdom of their own decisions. Your place is neither to follow them nor to change them. Your place is to make the best decisions you can for your own life, even if it means tiptoeing around your elders and their sensitivities.

Romeo and Juliet had it tough, with their families at war and their love explicitly forbidden. Any pressure you may face is probably a lot more subtle. "When are the two of you going to get married?" your mother may ask. Or maybe she doesn't even say it openly. You just see it in her eyes, her disappointment in you. It is like you're not a real grownup until you have joined the club. Then your mother can relax and stop worrying about you.

It is natural to want to please your parents. They made a

huge investment in you. Aren't you obligated to pay them back? Don't you have a responsibility to perpetuate their religion, family business, political beliefs and lifestyle? Centuries ago, the answer was unequivocally "Yes." If your father was a blacksmith, you would become one too. Modern cultures accept a different philosophy: that each person has the right of self-determination based on their own unique desires, skills and opportunities. The blacksmith may be disappointed that his son does not follow him, but no one outside the family would question the son's right to choose his own path.

Frankly, it is not possible to follow in your parents' footsteps even if you wanted to. Virtually everything about the world has changed in the 20-plus years since they were married. They alone insist that it hasn't, because they are deeply invested in the past world. They need to believe that what was good for them is good for you. They don't want to see you making a success of yourself doing the opposite of what they did, because then they would have to question their own decisions.

You are walking on eggshells here because you don't want to insult the people who raised you, but you also want to make wise choices for your own life, the vast majority of which will be conducted outside your elders' view. You can try to choose a life path that makes other people happy, but ultimately you are the one who has to live with it. If you buy something based on other people's needs and beliefs, not your own experience, you will probably end up with an inappropriate product that doesn't actually work for you.

The funny thing about social pressure is the people who are pressuring you will probably never be satisfied. If you get married as they want you to, it will keep them quiet for about a week. After that, they will come up with a new set of inadequacies you must repair, like "When are you going to have children?" If you address that demand, the next thing they will do is tell you how to raise those children. It is a fact of life: People who are unhappy will always be unhappy. If you let yourself become the instrument for making them happy, you are never going to win.

"When are you going to set down roots?" the elders may ask. This assumes that roots are necessary. Right now, you are an ambulatory animal, free to move and change as you wish. The elders want you to become a potted plant, stuck in one place and weighted down by obligations. It was good enough for them, so why isn't it good enough for you?

In traditional cultures, pressure to conform can be severe. In some countries you can't even be seen with a member of the opposite sex who isn't your relative, while homosexuality could get you killed. More liberal cultures may accept almost any lifestyle that doesn't hurt anyone else, but some form of social pressure is always present. It can simply take the form of you wanting to join the club everyone else has joined and make the others proud of you. A wedding is a bit like an award ceremony with others heaping praise, gifts and congratulations on you. Who doesn't want that sort of public affirmation?

In even the most liberal cultures, people must struggle with the existential conflict of Individual vs. Society. Society wants you to do things a certain way, based on a consensus of what works for everyone. That path, however, may not be what is best for you, because you have subtle and unique needs that society as a whole does not understand. If you have certain skills that few others have, the social norm may not be healthy for you. It is like pulling a mass-produced product off the shelf for a need that is deeply personal and not mass produced.

For example, if you are an average person, any kind of shoe will do. You can walk into any department store to buy them. If, however, you are a high-performance alpine mountain climber planning to scale Everest, you need a very special kind of shoe, and you need to test it carefully in the specialized environment in which you are working. You will devote a lot of time and money to finding the right footwear, and you will resist any attempt by others to impose their standard footwear on you. You don't climb Everest in a pair of sneakers, even if that's what everyone else in your family is wearing.

Relationships are like that: high-performance footwear for the specialized needs only you are facing. Unless you consider yourself an ordinary person with unambitious goals, no off-the-shelf solution will do and no pressure from others should make you accept one. Only you have to walk in those shoes. Only you plan to scale Everest in them.

What matters in the end is not how the shoes look to others but how they really work. For that, you need flexibility and the freedom to experiment. Every day, the shoes must prove themselves or you need another pair.

Personal Economies

Once upon a time, Europe got married. Over a dozen countries replaced their sovereign currencies with one common one, the Euro, as they merged their individual economies into a single mega-economy managed from Brussels. The new community would be much more efficient, the reasoning went. There would be no more patrolled borders, and all barriers to trade would be eliminated. People and goods would move easily between countries without any duties or inspections. Strong countries would pull up weaker ones, and all countries would equally share the burdens and responsibilities of the common good.

In contrast to its bloody history, Western Europe of the late 20th Century was finally at peace. War had been eliminated, and every country loved every other. Germany loved France who loved Italy who loved Spain. Why wouldn't they want to get married? It would give them all stability and security, they told themselves. It would prove their solidarity and cooperation. At the wedding, politicians made a lot of romantic speeches about how this marriage would change history and herald a brave new era of peace and prosperity. Only crabby old Britain had reservations. Its voters rejected the Euro and decided to keep their antiquated Pound. People called Britain stodgy and behind the times. Didn't it believe in love?

Turns out, Britain was the wiser one. The Euro marriage proved unhappy and imprudent—Big Time! It essentially gave weak and undisciplined countries like Greece a credit card based on the good credit of the stronger countries like Germany. Without any enforced constraints on its behavior, Greece happily maxed out its credit cards, buying an Olympics and lots of shiny new infrastructure it could never have afforded on its own.

Naturally, the bills came due, and Greece couldn't pay. This was a crisis not just for Greece but for all its marriage partners, because the healthy firewalls between their economies had been dissolved. They were all now in the same boat, furiously bailing, coping with the leaks the weaker countries created. The stronger countries had no choice but to continue covering for the weaker ones, because their own future was tied up with theirs.

Sound familiar? It is the story of a million marriages! If you remove healthy boundaries between two people, the weaker party is bound to draw down the stronger one. The stronger one will have little power to respond because his control has been diluted. The weaker one avoids direct responsibility for his actions because the stronger is always there to pick him up when he falls. This isn't just bad for the stronger party. The dysfunctions of the weaker are enabled by the common pot, allowing him to do more long-term damage to himself than he could have done on his own.

The Greek crisis would never have happened if Europe had not married. If Greece had remained single, the markets would never have allowed it to borrow as much as it did because its credit rating was so poor. Greece had poor credit for a reason: It was undisciplined. Europe couldn't make it more disciplined just by marrying it, although this was the belief at the time. Mainline Europe made the mistake of thinking it could change Greece's personality by devoting more love to it. Instead, it just released Greece from the immediate consequences of its actions.

If Greece had racked up unsupportable debt but remained single, it could have dealt with the crisis by devaluing its currency or defaulting on some of its debt. These would have been ugly solutions, roughly the equivalent of an individual declaring bankruptcy. There would have been plenty of pain, but only for Greece. The problems would have been resolved relatively quickly and Greece could have started over anew, as many Latin American countries did during their debt crises. These sovereign options were no longer possible after the marriage because the Greek economy was no longer an independent entity. It was part of a marriage community now, and everything one partner did intimately affected all the others.

At the time it got married, Europe failed to heed a universal truth: Individuals are defined by their economy. One of the things that makes Greece Greece and Britain Britain and you you and me me is our ability to manage our own checkbook. Every country and every adult human on Earth has the fundamental right and responsibility to balance their own budget. If you take this away, if you merge an individual's or country's financial life with that of another, they cease in many ways to be discrete beings. The community buffers them from the immediate consequences of what they do, so a lack of discipline and motivation is inevitable.

A country is not completely "real" unless it issues its own currency and controls its own borders. Otherwise, it is just lost in the soup of the community and has little control over its own fate. Because things are valued differently in different countries, you can't let goods and people cross from one to the other without some gatekeeping. What a lack of borders means in modern Europe is that if you want to smuggle contraband or people into Germany, you only need to get them past the weakest border of the weakest country. After that, you're home free!

Individuals do not issue their own currencies, but each person values money in their own way. It is unrealistic to think that two people can be completely in agreement on every expenditure. Some purchase that I think is worthwhile you may see as frivolous. This differing valuation does not have to come between us as long as we each control our own economy and suffer our own consequences for what we do. No matter how much I love you, how you spend your own money is simply none of my business. Merging our finances would be hurting our relationship, not helping it, because then your money is my money and we have to argue about every significant purchase, especially when money is tight.

When people get married, they may still maintain the illusion of independent finances. We can each have individual checking accounts and still hand each other cash. The trouble is, under marriage law, separate finances are a fiction. Creditors will still come after both of us for any unpaid bills and if there is a divorce, the spoils will be split evenly. Knowing something is fictional changes people's behavior. It's not the good times you have to worry about but the inevitable bad times, when money is tight and you are not in agreement on how to spend it. That's when one party starts drawing on the strength and good credit of the other and there's not a damn thing the other can do about it.

Money may seem crass and uncouth compared to love, but it is the primary regulating mechanism of the real world. It is nice when we can find non-financial ways to cooperate and get things done, but you dismiss the power of money only at your own peril. Money is a validation of your labor and a measure of your priorities. It is rarely distributed fairly, but to eliminate it would be even more unfair. No matter how strong your love may seem or how well-endowed your bank account, you will eventually have to pay bills, and you don't want the inevitable stresses of money to come between you.

To keep your love pure, you can't let money pollute it. The best way to protect your love is to retain the natural financial firewalls. Individuals must have borders just like countries. No matter how close we may be, there is a point where you end and I begin, and if you step over that line I'm going to bite your head off! A lot of the business of relationships is negotiating where that line should be, but it is nice to have a default line to fall back on.

If we remain single, the default financial borders are simple: My money and the things purchased with it are mine. Your money and the things purchased with it are yours. My assets do not become yours unless I write you a check or hand you some cash. My liabilities do not become yours unless you deliberately choose to contribute to them. You negotiate each case of sharing on its own merits. You don't share everything automatically all at once.

Greece was never a "bad" country, just a different kind of economy than Northern Europe. We all know people who plan ahead with their money and others who live from paycheck to paycheck. The paycheck people are no less noble; they just respond to a different set of financial incentives. It is like the difference between a Germanic culture and a Mediterranean one. Mediterraneans have always seemed more laid back, perhaps because they never had to plan for a harsh winter. That's part of their charm. Their personality works for them within the environment they create for themselves.

In a sense, Northern Europe created Southern Europe's woes by placing it in an environment of unlimited temptation where its natural system of controls no longer worked. By marrying the South with the noblest of sentiments, it upset its internal checks and balances. The North's responsibility is not diminished by the fact that the South wanted marriage too. It is like the crew of the Starship Enterprise violating the Prime Directive. You should avoid introducing your modern technology into weaker civilizations even if they want it, because any effort to "help" could have unintended negative consequences. They have to develop their own technology at their own pace, because then their culture has time to adjust to it.

A complete merging of economies is as unhealthy for individuals as it was for the Eurozone. That doesn't mean Europe won't work out its problems or that unstable marriages can't become stable with time, but the costs of integration can be huge and unnecessary. A merged economy is a ponderous and inflexible one, not nimble and adaptive, and if you erase too many borders between people, all sorts of diseases and dysfunctions can slip in. We can share some nice times together, but that doesn't mean we should share our whole immune system.

Why not just keep our finances separate and share only what we deliberately choose to share? Why do we need an absurd medieval institution to bind our financial lives together in a big pot? It doesn't make financial sense and does nothing to enhance our love. It is more likely to sabotage it.

Greece and Germany could have remained friends had they eschewed marriage and simply maintained their own separate economies. Instead of guaranteeing peace as it was supposed to do, marriage brought them to each other's throats and weakened both.

Being stranded in a lifeboat together, furiously bailing, is hardly romantic.

The Meaning of Life

When you have no meaning in your life and don't know what to do with yourself, you tend to look around at what other people are doing. Whatever activity they all seem to agree with, you follow along. "Maybe that will give my life meaning," you say, shrugging your shoulders.

What you may soon discover, though, is that none of those people you are following really know what they are doing either. They are just following the people who came before them. You may find too late that joining the pack doesn't really give your life lasting satisfaction. It only fills it up with obligations.

The alternative is to find your own direction and meaning. If you independently know who you are and where you are going, it is a lot easier to resist the siren's call of marriage and all the other traditions people follow without knowing why. But how do you find this direction?

In short, what is the meaning of life?

It is a question philosophers have been grappling with for ages. Let's see if I can knock it off in a few pages. This is my own theory, a simple default philosophy in case you can't think of another.

What is the meaning of life? There isn't any! At least there isn't any one universal truth we can all agree on. Religions claim to have a monopoly on truth, but their explanations seem to just go 'round and 'round. How do you know this path is the best? You just have to have faith, they say. I say no guru knows any more than any other. We have all been plunked down here on Earth without an instruction manual, and no one here has access to any special knowledge.

The only thing you know with reasonable certainty is life itself. Your own life. As you sit here reading this, you are occupying a body which seems solid and stable. Around you is a landscape filled with various objects and systems that also seem solid. Of course, it is possible that none of this is real. It could all be a virtual reality simulation inside an advanced supercomputer pumping inputs directly into your brain. (If you've seen *The Matrix*, you know the drill.) Nonetheless, this is still the best reality you have access to at the moment. You could call it "super virtual reality." No other reality is as complex, subtle and self-consistent as the one we were apparently born into, so we have to deduce and obey its rules.

One thing you learn pretty quickly about this reality is it can hurt. If you hold your hand above a candle flame, you will start to feel a profoundly unpleasant sensation that will probably linger long after you have pulled your hand away. That's called "pain." We all understand pain without reading any manual. It is an unpleasant sensation you want to avoid if at all possible.

There is nothing wrong with avoiding pain. In fact, you can build a pretty good working philosophy based on that alone. The complexity of this philosophy lies not in avoiding pain in the present but planning to avoid it in the future. This involves understanding the systems in which you find yourself enmeshed so you can predict how they will respond to your own behavior.

The more you learn about your world and the pain it can inflict, the more often you will find it best to endure a little pain now to avoid even greater pain in the future. For example, if you know a hard winter is coming, you will be willing to endure some discomfort and inconvenience in the summer to prepare for it. You stock up on supplies and mend the holes in your shelter.

Likewise, you should avoid the risk of catastrophic future pain whenever you can. Fastening your seatbelt may be annoying in the present, but it is better than smashing your face on the windshield at some unpredictable time in the future. You don't need a god to tell you these things, and you don't need a grand "meaning of life." All you need to know is that pain is unpleasant and potentially debilitating and should be avoided.

Pleasure follows different rules that are harder to pin down, but you know when something is pleasurable. It makes you smile, laugh and feel good about yourself. Pleasure differs from pain in that it is harder to reproduce. While holding your hand above a candle flame always produces the same pain, repeating the same formerly pleasurable activities rarely gives you the same degree of pleasant sensation. At best, you experience the curve of diminishing returns well known to drug addicts: The first hit is heavenly, the second okay, the third mediocre, until you are upping the dose to dangerous levels but still not reproducing your original high.

Some of the things that bring you pleasure have little to do with *you*, per se. A baby laughs when he learns something new or when he communicates with someone in a way he hasn't done before. An adult may feel good when someone they care about solves a painful problem. One thing that is reliably pleasurable for everyone is the sudden relief from long-term pain, but even that pleasure fades quickly as new problems inevitably replace the old.

Hedonists believe all that matters is pleasure and pain right now. Because they don't look very far ahead, they are trapped in a cycle of diminishing returns and repeated disasters they fail to anticipate. A more enlightened philosophy is *predictive* hedonism, where you try to anticipate what will cause you pleasure and pain in the future and plan accordingly. This is by no means an easy task. It requires constant inquiry into the nature of the world and your own internal systems. Since there is no simple rule for what is pleasurable, you have to experiment, see what works and deduce the higher-level rules by which it is governed.

Pleasure comes not just from serving your own needs. Helping others can also make you happy. To save someone from death or suffering usually makes you feel good. To not save them when you had the means to do so usually makes you feel bad. Seeing someone else in pain causes you pain, even when nothing has happened to you directly. You have a complex empathy formula to work out: How much pleasure or pain should you feel over the fate of others? If you are not responsible for everyone on the planet, who are you responsible for?

Once you decide that helping others is good for your own happiness, the question is how best to go about it. Should you use all your resources to feed the hungry, or should you try to address the underlying causes of hunger? Maybe hunger isn't even the best use for your limited resources. There is no sense on wasting energy on something you can have little impact on. Maybe there is something better you can do for others with the unique skills and resources you have.

I can't tell you what your goals should be. You have to find them yourself—then find them and re-find them again throughout your life.

Since pleasure in the same activities is rarely repeatable, you are pushed into progressively higher levels of accomplishment to maintain your own happiness. While an infant knows only his immediate environment, an adult should be gaining a wider perspective on how the world works and what his role in it is. The more you know, the more you can fine-tune or completely restructure your pleasure-seeking techniques. The tastes and goals of youth are bound to change as we gain more experience, but youth, with its current limited vision, cannot foresee how.

One thing that is usually pleasurable is successfully pushing your limits. There was something you thought you couldn't do. You saw others do it, but you were fearful and felt certain you didn't have the ability yourself. Then, after some experimentation and serendipitous discoveries, you find that you can do it after all. Maybe, to your surprise, you are quite good at it! You smile at that. It makes you happy!

Living alone might be one of those skills. Your fear of loneliness might be one of the things pushing you to get married. However, after being immersed in the needs of someone else, loneliness might actually start looking good. If you sample it again, maybe you will find that you didn't really need another person to make your life whole. Maybe all you really needed was more self-confidence. Once you have it, you can find pleasure in saying, "I can do this myself."

Happiness is a moving target. Just when you think you have it nailed down, it jumps to someplace else. At the same time, the thing you have nailed down becomes dead and meaningless—maybe even painful. That's why you have to avoid getting locked into grand long-term commitments. It is highly unlikely that pleasure will always move in the direction you have chosen. It is bound to change course. You can't know in advance how you will grow and change, so you have to leave yourself plenty of future maneuvering room. Decide what you need to decide right now, but leave the rest to be decided later.

Cracking the pleasure and pain code is probably the most challenging puzzle of life. You can never think you have "arrived" because that's when pleasure mysteriously vanishes. If you are open to it, you are bound stumble upon unexpected avenues for growth, and when you do, you need to be able to take them. It is much more complicated when you are traveling in twos, because the chance that your partner is ready to jump at the same time you are is very low.

A never-ending quest means ever-shifting alliances. People are important to you along your path of growth, providing examples, giving advice and serving as witnesses, but you can't say for certain that the same people will always be valuable to you. Indeed, some people may be pivotal in your life again and again, perhaps for a lifetime. You just can't predict which people it will be.

Choosing your fellow travelers should be simple. You just let the relationship decide itself, day by day, on its own merits. When it works, you stay together. When it doesn't, you draw apart. What is wrong with that?

The alternative is to handcuff yourself to one other person so neither of you has much choice about being there. You will probably find common ground with each other and "make it work," just like cellmates in prison. You certainly can't expect much growth out of it, though, compared to being free to choose.

If you truly love someone, why would you want to take away discretion? Isn't your love strong enough to stand on its own?

Death Benefits

Death can be very inconvenient, both for the person it happens to and the people left behind. No matter what you believe awaits you on the Other Side, it is clear that being dead greatly reduces your ability to interact with our current world. You can rattle your chains and haunt your old residence, but the chances of anybody listening and taking you seriously are slim.

It can be especially difficult to pass messages back to the living about what you want done with your estate and the important earthly projects you have been working on. Modern law and society expect you to have these matters settled *before* you depart this mortal plane. Seances have no validity in court!

Being dead may have its advantages. Hopefully, you will have no further worries and eternity will pass as painlessly as lounging on the beach in Fort Lauderdale. Your surviving partner, however, will continue to have worries, and it is a measure of your love right now that you anticipate what those worries may be and prepare for them as best you can. If you care about how they feel right now, then you should also care about their feelings and well-being after you are gone.

If you are romantically bonded with someone and have lived with them for a while, chances are you want the bulk of your estate to go to them. There are two reasons for this. First, you want your mate to have the means to continue without you. For example, if you have been sharing a house, and the house is in your name, you probably want them to have it so they can continue living there. Second, if your partner knows you better than anyone, they are best equipped to understand and implement your wishes. If they knew best what your goals were on earth, they would probably be in the best position to carry them on after you are gone.

It would be a great tragedy for your partner to be dedicated to you for years but have no control over your estate when you passed on. They would then be forced to negotiate with your parents, siblings or other relatives who would receive your estate by default. Those are people of your past who might not agree with your current goals to the same extent your partner does. Control of your legacy might be diluted, and the goals you fought for while alive could be sabotaged.

Death benefits are one area where marriage makes things easy. If you are married, the law automatically assumes your estate should go to your spouse. In addition, your spouse may continue to receive some of your retirement and pension payments (such as Social Security in the U.S.). If you remain alive but are unable to speak for yourself, your spouse has the greatest control over your care, and they would decide when to pull the plug after all hope is gone. Married people don't even have to make up wills, because all of these rights are automatically assumed under the law.

If you are not married to your partner, nothing is automatic and you must prepare for these circumstances with explicit legal contracts. Gay partners have learned how to do this in societies that don't allow them to marry, and heterosexuals would be wise to follow their lead. With the exception of certain retirement benefits, there are few rights conferred by marriage that can't be accomplished by separate legal contracts.

You must have a written will if you expect your unmarried partner to receive any part of your estate, and you must have a "living will" for them to have priority in caring for you when you are disabled. Once you believe you are in a stable relationship with someone, making up mutual wills should be one of your first legal steps together. You could even make a ceremony of it! Instead of say "'Till death do we part," you would be saying, "In death we shall be joined."

One benefit of having a will but not being married is that your surviving partner can receive your assets but doesn't have to accept any liabilities beyond the value of your estate. If you rack up huge uninsured medical bills in your final days, your married spouse would be responsible for paying them after your death. Your unmarried partner would not be. (Your estate could be charged for those bills, but your partner would not be obligated to pay what your estate cannot.) Likewise, if you were the subject of a lawsuit at the time of your death, the estate might bear continued liability, but your partner would not.

Furthermore, the beneficiary of your will has the right to *not* accept what you bequeath them. This is a subtle but sometimes important benefit. If I bequeath someone my pet elephant, perhaps as a cruel joke, they are not obligated to accept it, because the will is a one-way contract they never agreed to. If you bequeath something to your partner that is more a liability than an asset—like a heavily mortgaged house that needs repairs—your partner has the right to not accept it. This would not be true if you were married, where you have an equal interest in the house anyway.

Retirement benefits are more problematic. U.S. Social Security and most private pension benefits are transferrable only to married partners. Battling on the front lines, gays are making inroads in some states and countries, but governmental systems change very slowly. If you choose not to get married, you may have to face the fact that some of your partner's employment-related benefits may never be available to you.

A bigger moral question, though, is whether you *deserve*

the retirement benefits of your partner after they are gone. These benefits came about through their hard work, not yours. Pensions and employer-subsidized health insurance are the main tangible marriage benefits routinely denied to unmarried partners, but you could see these as more like corporate fringe benefits than natural, inalienable rights.

If you and your partner have become financially interdependent and you have no great assets to leave them, mutual life insurance policies may be the best solution, instead of or in addition to a will. Your partner's grief over losing you might never be erased, but a big check can make many practical problems easier. Grieving but rich beats grieving and destitute! Life insurance is especially important if you are raising children or have other joint projects together that you want to see continued.

Remember that legal responsibility for minor children is generally assigned by the birth certificate, not by the marriage contract. Whether you are married or unmarried, your legal and emotional obligations to your children remain the same, and you need to make provisions for them in case you pass on. These can include, in your will, an explicit statement of who you want your children to be raised by. This assignment is not absolute, but it is usually given weight by the courts.

Arranging to give your partner your assets after your death or incapacity is fundamentally different than irrevocably sharing them while you are both still alive, as in marriage. As long as you are conscious and unmarried, you have the power and responsibility to control your own assets and negotiate their distribution. If you and your partner truly love and trust each other, you are automatically going to share what you have, no contracts required. You don't have the legal obligation to share, but why do you really need it? Love alone should tell you what to share. If you don't like what you are getting or giving, then leave!

Death is a different circumstance because all negotiating power between the partners is now lost, and the unspoken trust you had when alive has little standing with the rest of the world. Now, the surviving partner is negotiating with courts, relatives, businesses and government agencies, and they need to have written evidence of the deceased's intentions.

A will is a relatively easy document to prepare. Do-it-yourself will kits are widely available and don't take long to complete—but you have to actually do it and not keep putting it off because you are both feeling healthy right now. Death and disability are notorious for turning up on your doorstep without an invitation.

Unlike marriage, a will is easy to revoke: You just tear up all copies of it or make up a new one to supersede it. You don't have to go to court or negotiate with your partner to dissolve a will; you just do it. If you remain unmarried, your assets remain yours to do with as you wish, before and after your death. Even if you are acting on whim, the decision to create, destroy or modify your own will is solely yours.

You probably want to consult with your beneficiary before you put them in your will, but there is no legal requirement to do so. Conversely, they have no obligation to accept what you bequeath them. This gives your partner a great deal of flexibility when you die. A will can give your partner most of the death benefits of marriage but with fewer obligations.

Ban Gay Marriage!
(heterosexual marriage, too!)
[From a satirical newsletter published by the author in 2008.]

It is a polarizing political question: Should committed gay and lesbian couples be allowed to legally marry? Should the institution be restricted to "one man and one woman," or can it also be "one man and one man"? For that matter, what about "one man and two women" or "one man, one monkey, three sheep and a donkey"? Where are we going to draw the line?

In my opinion, everyone has the question upside down. Instead of lobbying the legislature or sponsoring voter initiatives to promote one side or the other, we should be talking to each gay couple directly. We should be sitting them down, perhaps in a Christian setting, and counseling them on the facts of life.

Why would you want to screw up a perfectly good relationship?

Research shows that most divorces are caused by marriage. Furthermore, science can also prove that gay marriage will inevitably lead to gay divorce, just as nasty as the hetero kind.

Marriage, in fact, is downright dangerous. It's like handing out guns to teenagers. Who among us, when afflicted by love, has the mental capacity to comprehend "Til death do you part"? Who among us is truly competent to say, "I have thought through all the implications, and this is the only path I will ever want for the rest of my life?"

Gay couples don't know how good they got it! They can never make the Big Step. They can never go down to the Chapel of Love one drunken night and throw away all future discretion. They can never just close their eyes and jump.

They have to think things through. Due to the protective restrictions in current law, they can only take their relationship one step at a time, in a process resembling reason. They must explicitly choose to share property, death benefits and child custody on a thoughtful, case-by-case basis, not as a single blind package. Yes, there are still a few retirement benefits that gay couples can't share, but most marriage services are available á la carte to anyone with some creativity.

Pity the poor heterosexual couple, living together in sin. To them, marriage is always the elephant in the room, the dark cloud hanging over their heads. When the relationship isn't perfect and you wonder what's wrong, it is easy to think that a lifetime contract must be the missing piece.

You can ask a divorcee: When did the relationship start to fall apart? A common reply is: "On the day we got married." Most relationships don't need and can't support the whole marital package. The most dangerous part is that individuality and self-responsibility often get suppressed, setting the stage for an explosion later on.

If you truly love someone and want to be with them, then why do you need the contract? If you are drawn together, so be it; if you grow apart, then you split up. Isn't the government contract, and all the economic and social baggage it carries, getting in the way of your free expression? If you're unmarried and you stay together, you know it is love. If you're encumbered and you stay together, you can never be sure.

If your particular insanity is to lust after the opposite sex, then government should tolerate your personal preference, but it doesn't need to sanction it. Marriage is, in essence, a form of religious expression that government ought to stay jolly well clear of.

Who is behind the marriage conspiracy? It's the Big Corporations, of course! They have fed us this delusion for years, because they know it is easier to sell useless products to trapped married people.

Only the gays are still free.

Addendum 1:
The Istanbul Interview

Following is an interview conducted with the author in December 2012, coinciding with release of the Turkish-language translation of this book (which was published before the English edition).

What motivated you to start writing about marriage?

I had been through my own marriage and divorce, and I can say I was totally unprepared, both for how my marriage unfolded and the difficult way it ended. The way I dealt with my own Post Traumatic Stress is I went to the local divorce court in Las Vegas and started looking at the whole legal system of marriage and divorce. I sat in on a lot of other people's divorce cases as a sort of entertainment and this made me see how deluded people are about marriage when going into it. You fully understand marriage, the full legal aspects of it, only when you are getting divorced. After a while, the idea for this book started to take shape, mainly inspired by my study of divorce court.

Because your own marriage did not go well, couldn't we say that you have a personal grudge against marriage and this is coloring your perception?

I don't think so. First of all, my own marriage was long over when I started writing. It was some years later, so it's not like I was out for vengeance. It was mainly watching other people's divorces that inspired me. Divorce is really fascinating, because that's when all the bills come due. All the delusions you had when you got drawn into marriage come back to bite you in the end.

What did you think about marriage before you got married?

I thought it wouldn't make much difference. In America, we have relatively liberal attitudes toward people living together, so there's really nothing you can do when you are married that you can't do when you are single. I thought marriage was just a legal and social convenience. We wouldn't have to make out separate wills, for example, and I could refer to my partner as my "wife" instead of my girlfriend. What I didn't realize is that we were also merging our financial lives in a way that ultimately wasn't healthy. In many ways, this simple legal distinction changed our relationship immensely and not in a good way.

I must confess that my beliefs about marriage before I got into it weren't entirely consistent. One side of my brain was thinking, "This won't make any difference," but the other side was thinking, "OK, this legitimizes our relationship. It must be real now."

Can we ever talk about a thing such as "good marriage"?

Of course! There are good relationships and many that last a lifetime. But it isn't the institution of marriage that makes them that way. If marriage didn't exist, these relationships would still be strong.

Have there ever been any free relationships in history? Was marriage always the only option?

We don't have much history to work with! The world even fifty years ago was a much different one. The main change is birth control. Throughout most of human history, having sex meant having babies, and a society had to have a mechanism to assure that young people didn't have sex or babies randomly. You needed this institution of marriage to assure, for example, that a man didn't abandon the woman he impregnated and that stable conditions were in place to raise the child. Marriage was a perfectly logical process in, say, medieval Europe. If you wanted to have sex you had to be prepared for the babies that followed and this meant a stable, socially sanctioned relationship with the blessings of the community.

Today, marriage and childrearing are almost completely separate issues. At least in America, if a man fathers a child, his legal responsibilities for it are exactly the same regardless of whether the couple is married. Either you're in the household helping to support the child or you are paying child support. Your marital status has nothing to do with it. So the original purpose of marriage is now gone, yet people still get married. Why do they still do it? I think it's delusion. People think that by joining this ten-thousand-year-old tradition they are somehow improving their lives and improving the relationship, which simply isn't true.

Everything around us points to marriage. Most religions, ideologies, art, culture and traditions seem to encourage it. Under such conditions, how do we struggle against this giant institution?

I'm not in the business of struggling against giant

institutions. I don't care about changing the Catholic Church, the government of Turkey or any other institution. In all of my writings, I'm only speaking to you, the reader. Regardless of what institutions do or say, no one has more control over your life than you do. All I want to do is show you how your own thinking may be flawed, as mine was.

We know that millions of people suffer in their marriages. What should married people do to get out of this trap, as soon as they realize it is a trap?

I don't have an easy answer to that. That's exactly the dilemma I was facing when I was married. I knew, early on, that the marriage wasn't working, but my sense of obligation kept me in it. I not only had my wife to think about but also her children from previous marriages who I had vowed to support. I hung on to the bitter end, trying desperately to make it work. I would not have filed for divorce if I thought there was any other option. But after I took that step and dealt with the consequences, I realized that divorce was much healthier for both of us and that my holding on for so long really caused a lot of damage. My most important advice is that if divorce is going to happen, it should be done soon and quickly. It doesn't serve anyone to drag it out.

Previous marriages? You mean you married a woman who had been married more than once before? Shouldn't that have been a warning to you?

I think so! I laugh about it myself. But when one is in love, one doesn't think rationally. We all know this. People in love are not sane. They are the worst people to be making fateful choices about lifetime commitments.

Should marriage be totally abolished?

Of course not. Marriage is part of our culture and is here to stay. It's just one of the ways people organize themselves. You wouldn't try to abolish marriage any more than you would try to abolish a religion you didn't agree with. Marriage is one option society offers you. You either take it or you don't.

What options do we have for the relationship if we don't get married?

I can only speak about America, not any other country. In America, virtually every benefit of marriage is available to unmarried couples. You can still have sex and live together. You can still have children. You can make up wills, buy life insurance and list each other as beneficiary. You can buy real estate and open bank accounts together. You can pick and choose any options of marriage that you want. The only difference is you are doing it deliberately in a step-by-step process, not all at once in a single step. Anything that you don't explicitly decide to share remains your own individual property.

In America, the only benefits couples still can't get when unmarried are the sharing of certain health insurance and retirement plans. You also can't get your foreign partner American citizenship if you aren't married. I think it is questionable whether couples are naturally entitled to these benefits anyway. You'll take them if available, but I don't think the Bible ever said anything about immigration and health insurance.

Otherwise the only practical difference between being married and unmarried is whether you choose to connect yourself with another person slowly and deliberately, thinking about each step, or whether you do it all at once, in a single ceremony, not fully understanding all the effects.

What are the unbearable times of a marriage?

The most unbearable times in a marriage are when you can't say what you are really thinking because you know your partner will blow up. With time, the areas you can't talk about get bigger and bigger, until you are hardly saying anything at all.

Even those who are critical of marriage (feminists, some leftists) do get married at the end. What do you think is the reason for that?

It is extremely difficult to resist this calling. Marriage is the elephant in the room in any relationship. Everyone is looking for approval from others, and marriage seems to provide it. It seems like you don't have to explain yourself anymore. You're just "husband and wife." There is also a great temptation to believe, when your relationship isn't progressing, that marriage is going to somehow improve things. It doesn't improve anything, but people still think, "Why not give it a try? It seemed to work for my parents and my grandparents and my great-grandparents, so why not me?" What you don't realize is these people were living in an entirely different world than we are today. We have more freedom today and that means more responsibility. You don't blindly choose your parents' way of life any more than you would blindly follow their career path.

If you have already been living together with your partner for years, have already worked out all your boundary issues, and you decide to make it "official" with a marriage ceremony, you can invite me and I won't object. The mistake is thinking that marriage itself can improve your relationship or help you work out your issues. If there are any problems in your relationship, marriage is going to make them worse, not better.

In Turkey and in many other societies there is what we call "marriage pressure" from one's family. How can one struggle against that?

In America, there isn't the same sort of family pressure there is in Turkey. I'm not saying it isn't there; it's just much more subtle. In America, you now can openly live with your partner, of any gender, without shame and with full acceptance from society. When there is marriage pressure in America, it is usually from parents who are recent immigrants to the country from more traditional societies.

In a sense, though, we all face social pressures to live our lives in certain ways. If it isn't explicit pressure—"When are you going to get married?"—then it's subtle and implicit pressure. I know there are some societies where you are virtually forced to get married, but I don't think Turkey is one of these. You still have the choice. Your family won't disown you if you don't get married. You just have to decide whether you want to put up with the flak you get from them whenever you get together.

The important thing to remember is this is your life, not theirs. Whatever decisions you make, you're the one who has to live with them. You don't want to do something to make your parents happy for a few minutes but have to live in misery for years. The funny thing about family pressure is it never seems to go away no matter what you do. Once you do one thing to make your family happy, they are still unhappy and want you to do something else. If you get married, the next pressure is, "Why aren't you having children?" That's another big issue. Thanks to birth control, these are choices that previous generations didn't have, and you have to make them yourself based on your own personal judgment. You can't let your family make these decisions for you.

There is the claim that commercial capitalism encourages loneliness so that it can sell more products. What do you think?

Maybe it's the opposite. Sometimes I think capitalism wants you to be married so you're trapped in a home and they can sell you more useless stuff. Honestly, though, capitalism is the most liberal force in the universe. They will go wherever the money is. If there are a lot of gay unmarried couples in the community, capitalism will find ways to sell them things. Capitalism isn't like religion with a fixed set of rules. Capitalism goes with the flow.

How does marriage affect the children? And can unmarried partners easily handle the children if they have independent lives?

One of the reasons I got married is we were raising children together and I thought marriage would somehow make it easier. What I've learned since then is marriage has nothing to do with child rearing, legally or practically. In America, I know many unmarried couples who are raising children. There is still a mom and a dad—or two moms or two dads. One of them usually spends more time with the children and the other usually works more. They are both home at night and live in an arrangement that looks a lot like traditional marriage. They just haven't taken the legal step of getting married. If you ask them why they are not married, they say, "We have never seen the need for it."

If you are dedicated to your partner and your children, then you don't need marriage to tell you how to behave. On the other hand, if your relationship falls apart, or one biological parent refuses to support the children, than there is a legal mechanism for that, called child support. In America, child support is a completely separate legal issue from marriage, even though they are usually handled at the same time in divorce proceedings. If you made the children, then you are legally responsible for supporting them, regardless of your marital status.

As for the children's emotional health, I don't think marital status matters to them either. It matters to them whether Mommy and Daddy love each other or Mommy and Daddy are always fighting and can't talk to each other. That is pretty much independent of marital status, except that when people are married, they are under more social and financial pressure to stay together when they no longer belong together.

But shouldn't a relationship have some rituals which mark certain milestones?

I say rituals are dangerous! You don't need milestones. Your love alone should be enough. I say that if you truly love someone, are truly attached to them, then your love alone is enough to keep you together. You make the free-will decision every day to stay together. Marriage is just a complication, erasing too many of the healthy boundaries between you and essentially forcing you together a times when you don't belong together.

Every relationship has its ups and downs. There are times you draw close to each other and times you want to pull away. This is natural. Marriage, by merging all your accounts at once, makes it harder to pull away when you should. It's like handcuffing yourself to your partner. Love is no longer a free-will choice. If you think handcuffs strengthen your love, you are wrong. They just make love harder to prove.

Considering the Western societies, how do you see the future of marriage? The latest statistics show that an increasing number of adults now cohabitate or live alone; is marriage finally being called into question?

I don't deal in statistics. I don't care what the great mass of humanity is doing or whether marriage is rising or falling in popularity. All that really matters is you and me.

I do care about freedom, that a society allows people to make their own choices about how to live their own lives. America has become very liberal about this. America hasn't always been liberal, but it has been relatively quick to change. Some places like Iran are still very conservative where you have little freedom. I see Turkey as somewhere in-between. There are a lot of things we may not like about our society, but the important thing is whether we can find an accommodation in it, find some little corner where we can quietly live as we choose.

Addendum 2:
100 Tweets on Marriage

Some things are best said in few words. That must be why God invented Twitter, where all messages must be 140 characters or less. Below are one hundred of the author's tweets on marriage and relationships (tweeting as @BadDalaiLama). Here you will find concise statements of many of the ideas discussed in this book, as well as a few thoughts on relationships in general.

1. Trying to capture love with marriage is like displaying a wild animal on your wall. As soon as you've nailed it down, you've killed it.

2. Beauty cannot be purchased or possessed. If you try, all you'll get is bragging rights to the beauty that was once there.

3. As a rule, Paradise turns into Hell as soon as you move there.

4. If you're not willing to fight, stand up for your interests and defend your borders, then love is not the place for you.

5. Love alone cannot bear the weight of all we ask it to do.

6. Given the credit card of life, most spend it to the max as soon as they can, laboring the rest of their lives to pay the interest.

7. A relationship cannot truly grow unless there is the realistic option to withdraw and renegotiate.

8. A romantic relationship should not be confused with a parental one.

9. A successful relationship isn't merging. It is sharing of independent viewpoints.

10. Don't be a victim of your own cleverness—finding ingenious ways to sustain a relationship that really should end.

11. Even after years of research and testing, there is still no clean-burning form of love.

12. Every relationship is a balance between sharing and the need to preserve ones own identity.

13. You can't prove love by killing freedom.

14. If a little of something makes you happy, that doesn't necessarily mean a lot of the same thing will make you more happy.

15. A bad marriage is the ultimate police state, with Big Brother watching your every move for signs of disloyalty.

16. Love is not a steady state but an ongoing negotiation to get what we want.

17. Adult personality cannot be changed from the outside, especially within the scope of romance. Change may happen, but only after you're gone.

18. Love is a means of travel, not a destination.

19. People in love are not sane. They are the worst people to be making fateful choices about lifetime commitments.

20. It is remarkable how humans can willingly accept imprisonment in exchange for the approval of their family and society.

21. Failed romances are one of life's great classrooms. You learn how people really work and how fantasy differs from fact.

22. Gay couples who cannot marry must take their relationship in small discretionary steps in a process resembling reason.

23. Falling in love with someone is the best guarantee that you won't be able to change them.

24. Love is a condiment of life, not a main course. It can't give you a meaningful mission any more than ketchup is a food group.

25. Given the choice between being lonely and losing yourself in a relationship, lonely gives you far more options.

26. Love is a dance of "Closer, please, but not too close!"

27. It is remarkable how love can turn lead into gold—and back to lead again shortly after marriage.

28. Romantic love is a partnership, not a charity. You're not there to repair the other person or protect them from themselves.

29. Happiness is not a permanent condition. It must be constantly renegotiated and cannot be nailed down in the future by any form of contract.

30. Hubris is thinking your romance will last forever.

31. It is plain enough to us when a friend gets drawn into an unproductive relationship. If only we had that same insight for ourselves

32. Marriage is like giving guns to teenagers. Who among us, in the heat of passion, can comprehend the implications of "Til Death Do You Part"?

33. Romance does not just combine the strengths of two people, also their weaknesses.

34. If a relationship is faltering, don't fool yourself into thinking you need "more commitment" and fewer options for escape.

35. The main effect of marriage is to tie people together by shared financial obligations. This is different than being tied together by love.

36. The neutralizing of future discretion should not be mistaken for a declaration of love.

37. In Medieval times, marriage was a necessity. You couldn't have sex, live together or have children without it. Today it is a vanity.

38. The unmarried look longingly over the fence at those who are married. The married look longingly back.

39. Marriage can give you a front-row seat to insanity no one else can see.

40. In the beginning, love is defined for us by others. We have to fail many times before we learn to define it for ourselves.

41. Romance is a futile attempt to reproduce the apparent security and unconditional love of childhood.

42. It's a bad sign for your relationship if you're watching your words and editing your thoughts to not trigger an explosion.

43. Ice is water that got married. Those free-flowing days are over!

44. Instead of making one grand decision based on faith, you should make many small decisions based on knowledge.

45. In every relationship, you have to fight for what you want, especially from those you love.

46. The greatest wealth is the freedom to change.

47. Just because you love someone doesn't mean you can live with them.

48. It doesn't say much for your relationship if you think you need marriage to lock you in and make it harder to escape.

49. If one fat person marries another, they'll both get REALLY fat. Same with any other mutual defect.

50. Looking back on our own romantic obsessions, we are bound to exclaim, "I can't believe I fell for that!"

51. Loss of libido is a crisis only if you are already committed to a relationship that depends on it.

52. Gays battling for the right to marry is like men fighting for the right to wear corsets.

53. Love is harmless. The obligations that follow on its heels are not.

54. Loyalty isn't all that admirable if it makes you hold on to a dysfunctional relationship.

55. Making babies is the standard turnkey solution for couples who can't think of anything else to use their relationship for.

56. Many a marriage is kept marginally afloat by the herculean efforts of one party who mistakenly takes the wedding vows literally.

57. Romance is powered by the need to believe, which can sweep all sorts of disturbing evidence under the carpet.

58. In any relationship, how you argue is more important than what you argue about.

59. You can't reason with the gambler, the addict or someone in love. They may agree with your logic, but it won't change their behavior.

60. In romance, you build the theatre, write the script, choose your own role and cast a lead actor. Don't rant at all actors if the play sucks.

61. Marriage is the most effective Redpill you can take. In a few weeks you'll start seeing your partner for who they really are.

62. In any relationship, there are times you draw close and times you pull away. You damage the former if you try to prevent the latter.

63. Marriage, under the law, has nothing to do with love. It is an economic incorporation that most relationships are much healthier without.

64. Much of what we call romance is the attempt to outsource responsibility for our own life.

65. If you grew up in a paper mill town, the smell of wet paper would remind you of home and you'd probably marry someone who smelled like that.

66. Love without flowers, chocolate, jewelry, children, alcohol, codependency or interior decorating. Can you imagine such a thing?

67. Marriage and home improvement recursively justify each other.

68. In romance, you are not a therapist, protector or parent. You are a consumer, willing to pay a reasonable price for a quality product.

69. Even a "successful" marriage runs the risk of freezing your life in place and bringing an end to creative growth.

70. Only in romance are people expecting someone else to save them from themselves.

71. Passion alone cannot fuel a long-term relationship.

72. People in love build a mythology about their early days that involves some selective memory loss. When love ends, full memory comes back.

73. Marriage is most destructive when you have to mute your own growth to match that of your jealous and less competent partner.

74. The recurring error of investors everywhere is to take the "trend" of today and extrapolate it in a straight line into the future.

75. People tend to confuse having a lot of obligations with having a meaningful life, so they pile on the obligations.

76. Relationships are damaging when they disrupt the individual's direct negotiation with outside reality.

77. Romantic love is a value-added service. If you are not receiving value in excess of the price paid, you shouldn't be using the service.

78. Most forms of mutual protection become unequal over

time, with one party giving far more than he is getting.

79. Romantic relationships are successful only when power is relatively equal and each person remains responsible for their own problems.

80. single — adj. the state of being able to do whatever you want with your life without having to negotiate with anyone.

81. Someone in love is the perfect propagandist, trumpeting the positive aspects of their choice while obscuring the negative.

82. Survival in marriage means carefully watching your words and not rocking the boat.

83. Romance involves the acceptance of creeping change, often leading to conditions you never would have agreed to in the beginning.

84. The dueling agendas of gay rights are "Government must stay out of our bedroom," and "Government must sanction our relationship."

85. The greatest danger of marriage is the loss of negotiating power.

86. The main fallacy of romance is thinking someone else can give your life meaning when you can't find it yourself.

87. When your love is completely selfless, prepare to be abused.

88. The only thing sadder than divorce is a failed marriage that does not end.

89. The premise of many a Hitchcockian thriller—and countless real-life ones—is how your partner changes after you are married.

90. You don't fall in love with a person but with an image of them which is partly a fiction in your own mind.

91. The scary thing about intimate relationships is how one party accepts and adopts the dysfunctions of the other.

92. There are no unconditional relationships. You have to

Glenn Campbell

fight for what you want, even from those you love.

93. To be against marriage doesn't mean you are against love. It only means you don't want money to come between you.

94. Walking down the aisle, taking the marriage vows, the bride is thinking: "What does everyone think of me? Am I doing this right?"

95. We design our own romantic disasters. The opposite gender just fulfills them for us.

96. When you find something thrilling, the worst thing you can do is commit yourself to repeating it. The thrill goes, but the commitment stays.

97. You never know what a person is really like until after the honeymoon.

98. Young people in love think they have things all worked out, but time will teach them otherwise.

99. Your best asset in romance is to not really need it.

100. Free will dies the moment you say "forever".

For links to the author's other work, including his popular social media accounts, see his website at Glenn-Campbell.com

Acknowledgements

I am grateful to Cemal Atila, my Turkish publisher, for rescuing this manuscript from obscurity and inspiring me to complete it.

www.ingramcontent.com/pod-product-compliance
Lightning Source LLC
Chambersburg PA
CBHW022334280326
41934CB00006B/631